THE LAD FROM SPARKBROOK

Comical and candid tales of an Irish upbringing in post WWII Birmingham, England

Martin McEvilly

McEvilly Publications Limited

Authors note

This written work is the first book by myself, Martin McEvilly. Several chapters of the book were written when I was suffering and successfully overcoming Corona Virus. After twenty-three days I displayed the first signs of recovery by being able to put on my own socks and so decided to finish the story.

I dedicate this book firstly to my parents my mother Mary-Kate Atkinson and my father James Patrick. No words will ever be able to describe how grateful I am for my parents, both immigrants, for never displaying weakness when working 7 days a week to keep eight children on the straight and narrow. I also dedicate this book to my brother Seamus who fell at the first hurdle in life.

This books is mostly written as my young eyes saw Sparkbrook in the post WWII, where I grew up. It hopefully shows an insight into an Irish family upbringing in Birmingham and also the wide ethnic diversity that came with immigration which has made me who I am today. It is written with fond memories of all its characters (mostly) and isn't intended to offend or insult anyone. Some names have been changed for the purpose of narrative.

CONTENTS

CHAPTER 1 :
SPARKBROOK

Sparkbrook. An inner-city area in southwest Birmingham, England, is one of four wards forming the Hall Green district within Birmingham City Council. The area received its name from the Sparkbrook, a stream that flowed south of the City centre. Later it was channelled and partially used for a canal — the areas which envelopes Sparkbrook are the districts of Sparkhill, Small Heath and Digbeth. My parents had moved there in 1951 from a slum dwelling in Edgbaston, a district divided by class, wealth and poverty. Both my parents were economic migrants from the West Coast of Ireland and, fortunate to secure themselves a back to back end terrace property where seven families shared a single toilet. Access to these houses was via an arched narrow eroded brick-clad entrance with house number seven located at the top of the open alleyway. I was fortunate not to have experienced the deprivation and poverty of number seven at the rear number six Great Colmore Street, but my elder brother and sisters did.

Since the Second World War up to the early sixties, the areas of Sparkhill and Sparkbrook had taken in thousands of economic and displaced immigrants from war-ravaged countries such as Ireland, Poland, Southern Italy and Eastern Europe. Between the early sixties and the late sixties, numerous new types of immigrants moved into the twilight area of Sparkbrook. These new kinds of immigrants invited to live and work in the United Kingdom by the then Conservative Government to fill the skills and cheap labour shortages arising from the aftermath of the Second World War. This experiment you could say was Britain's embryonic step towards globalisation. The second wave of mass immigration into the Sparkbrook district brought its peculiarities and inherent problems. The commonwealth immigrants, especially those from Pakistan broadly known as the subcontinent were of different colour, language, religion, appearance and they consumed completely different food tasting and smelling differently to the food the Irish cooked and ate. They would sometimes wear their cultural clothes on Friday, which they called 'shalwar kameez'.

This dress displayed their culture and religion as every Friday they would gather in a mosque and pray together in the afternoon. Their taste buds were more toward the spicy and oily side, which was different from the Irish liking. Some religious folks would gather in a mosque and pray five times a day. During their holy month of Ramadan, they would fast for the whole month. In the end, they would celebrate their fast like Christmas, but they called it Eid. They had different skills in terms of employment and found it challenging to engage with their white immigrant predecessors. Indians had the same observational strictures with the exception they were more approachable and had a liking for alcohol. Indians culture was similar because, at that time, both these countries were newly formed due to the partition of the subcontinent. However, religiously, they were very different from Pakistanis as they followed Hinduism while the majority of Pakistanis were Muslims. Indians would celebrate on occasions like Diwali etc. Indian wives would fast for their husbands on a special day. Due to religion, some Indians would not eat beef. While a few would not even eat meat of any kind, they were vegetarians. When they would go to visit their temples, they would prepare some sweets to give to everyone to eat. Some Indians called Sikhs wore Turbans and occasionally dressed traditionally, which was always a delight to see and were allowed to drink alcohol during party time. Sikhs were religiously different from Hindus. They followed their religion called Sikhism. While Hindus believed in polytheism, Sikhs believed in monotheism, and they followed Baba Guru Nanak Dev. The Pakistanis could not drink alcohol in pubs, bars etc. while Hindus could not eat meat but could enjoy drinking and Sikhs would do both. Their specific dish was called 'Palak paneer'.

The African and Caribbean immigrants, in contrast, had darker skin, whiter teeth with gold fillings wore with great pride suits similar to demob suits and donned large felt trilby hats. They ate an awful amount of jerk chicken meals with Yam. Whenever they cooked, you could always smell ginger, chillies garlic and lots of other spices and ingredients, which were alien to the Irish palate. Whenever they could afford to buy a car, they would purchase a large saloon car like a Ford Zephyr or a ford Zodiac with cushions covered in tiger skin placed in the rear window of a car, which received the habitual Saturday wash. Carribean immigrants were very similar to the Irish who didn't care who ruled the world so long as the party had plenty of food, drink, music and of course work to be had.

My young ears would hear their language called 'patois', which was difficult to understand for most Irishmen and Africans. Their culture mainly consisted of drum and deep base driven music mixed with spicy food. They would enjoy music to the fullest extent whether they were drinking at a party or praying in a church. The majority of African and Caribbean families would dress up on Sunday mornings and take their children to a place of worship where loud clapping and gospel singing took place for most of the morning. I noticed they always appeared to enjoy life to the fullest and the new world around them in England.

CHAPTER 1 : 3
PALMERSTON ROAD

The house I was born in was a double fronted mid terraced property situated on the bend of Palmerston Road. It had a double front door and an opening to a small hallway. Behind the double external doors was a short hallway with a colourful tiled floor leading to another entrance, a single door with a large bright stained-glass pane. The symmetry of our house allowed two reception rooms, one dining room and a kitchen on the ground floor. The second floor had three bedrooms, one bedroom for my parents, one bedroom for my sisters and another bedroom for the boys. It also had a large bathroom and, with this came a staircase leading to the attic floor having a narrow landing approach which widened to allow you entry to two large attic bedrooms where at times up to four lodgers would stay. The garden to the rear was relatively narrow with an outside brick toilet linked to the house adjoining a rectangular shed. During the summer months, the shed house chickens and their chicks. At the bottom of the garden, there was a garage large enough to accommodate three saloon cars. Included in the garage area was a space for Dads' workbench and whatever timber he managed to transport home from building sites using his A35 Austin van and its roof rack.

My father like most immigrants worked hard to better himself and, made money demolishing Anderton Air Raid Shelters which meant he could afford to purchase a better and bigger house in Sparkbrook, a far cry from the misery of Great Colmore Street. Within weeks of moving into the new address, he managed to procure a giant beer barrel from the local brewers called Mitchells and Butlers and sawed the barrel into two halve, turned them upside down and planted his favourite Geraniums plants. My mother would complain about Dad having more consideration for his Geraniums in half barrels and the Rhododendrons in the hanging baskets than he did his family. I suppose being born and raised on a farm afforded him a special dispensation to be closer to nature. I never knew my green-fingered father to grow any form of plant or vegetable without complete success. Every year Dad would forget his building commitments and return to the farm in Plovervale to Mayo to be with all his mother. Sometimes he would go off shooting with his brother. With safety uppermost in his mind, he would send us to Grandma Atkinsons in Ballavary for the day, out of harm's way. In the evening we'd return to the farmhouse in Plovervale to watch Dad skinning rabbits and plucking feathers from the days shooting of game.

Every school day morning noisy idling diesel engines outside my bedroom woke me up. The noise sometimes increased with the sound of loud voices speaking English with a heavy brogue. This event took place at six-thirty every morning, six days a week, fifty-two weeks a year. Immediately outside the door on the other side of our road stood a line of green and brown coloured wagons with company logos painted on the doors, displaying predominantly Irish names. These wagons first duty would be to ferry Irish labourers to their job site in and around and sometimes beyond the city boundaries for the day. The second time I would wake up was when I could hear the sound of men's studded steel toe capped boots scrapping the blue paviours of Palmerston road. These men travelled from Connaught and other regions of the Irish free state to work as navvies on British building sites. They came from large Catholic Irish families struggling to survive on small rented farms.

Paradoxically, they came to help the country their grandfathers fought for in South Africa against the Boers. When their fathers returned home, they discovered their families evicted from their rented homes and farms by greedy English Protestant landlords. They replaced the starving families with Protestant families, and the majority of the Irish Catholic families were allowed to starve to death with many seeking passage to America or Australia unless of course, they resentfully conceded to the joining Protestant faith with a bribe of 'taking the soup'.

Years of heavy manual outdoor labouring morphed into weathered red faces; nicotine-stained fingers; powerful claw-like hands; long sideburns and strong, broad shoulders. With their thumbs tucked into trousers, they walked up the short Palmerston Road hill to join a line of men with their backs against a brick wall facing opposite our house. Most conversations described the previous day's work experience. Stories of unscrupulous employers ferrying labourers to the other side of the city as far away as Wolverhampton and setting them to work by giving them money to pay for breakfast. Having had breakfast and worked hard all day, they discovered their employer for the day had abandoned them, leaving them to find their way home with no money. Somehow, this act of callousness failed to damper their spirits and raised voices could be heard the following morning with exchanges of banter over Gaelic football teams and whether men from Mayo were better workers than men from Galway. Men from the west considered themselves better and more robust than men from affluent counties surrounding Dublin. Dublin men were always called the narrow backs because of their size and reluctance to work hard manually. The majority of these immigrants had ambitions, dreams that encourage the spirits of most immigrants to continue. That dream was to return home to their farm in Ireland with a ball of money in their pockets. Many had worked for the British for many years.

CHAPTER 1 : HONEST WORKING MEN

The securing of decent days pays for honest days' work meant adopting a procedure. This procedure involved a man approaching the quasi labour exchange, a labour exchange uniquely different from any other labour exchange of its day. Men stood with their backs against a wall, caps in their hands waiting for a ganger man. During the cold winter labourers would jostle and tussle to the front to be chosen first as this meant they could travel in the wagon cabin with the driver and ganger man. However, those who were not so lucky would travel on a bench inside the unsecured canopy which meant sitting there for maybe forty minutes in the bitter cold playing twenty-five the Irish card game with arbiter rules. The real men would stand outside and grip the canopy with all the strength they had in their fingertips with shirts openly displaying their hairy chests. A real west of Ireland man would never sit inside a canopy. It was more macho for a man to bear his chest no matter what the weather. Sometimes those men who failed the interview and ironically missed the delightful cold journey to work could be heard shouting back at the foreman.

"Boots or no boots. I will be there in the morning."

Failure to obtain a shift for the day meant a man went back to his lodgings for the morning and then down to the Public House only the Irish would frequent. Such Pubs would always be busy on a Monday. Full to the brim with strong, healthy men unable to rise from their beds due to drinking late on Sunday night or merely unwilling to show enough eagerness to prepare a clean pair of steel toe-capped boots and wide leather belts with large buckles supporting corduroy trousers and, of course, a flat cap. These gentlemen were known as the honourable members of the Monday club.

On Sunday, the very same men would attend mass at the local Catholic Church wearing dark suits, clean white-collar shirts and a trilby hat. There were two prominent churches within the immediate area of Sparkbrook. One was called Saint Anne's, which was within the parish of Digbeth close to the city centre and, the other was called English Martyrs. This church you would find by walking up the Stratford road to Sparkhill. English Martyrs was infinitely more popular than Digbeth because there were more priests, the sermon was shorter and, there was a choice of several more pubs within walking distance.Every Sunday priests of the parish would reserve some of the sermons to admonish unnamed members of the congregation. A stern message during their rambling epistle was necessary because some members of the congregation failed to listen when lectured to by the priest that it was not a Christian act to leave the weekly mass and walk into the nearest pub and drink until closing time. Many of the heathens would slurp a gallon of pints, smoke packets of untipped Senior Service cigarettes and then head off for more entertainment at Glebe farm about five miles away. Glebe farm was a municipal park comprising several Gaelic football pitches and one for Hurley. The playing pitches where the Finnian battle sites where a man could let off all the steam he wanted.

The steam built up over the previous week's alcoholic excesses, listening to the wife, screaming kids and having to endure consecutive days of hard manual work in the trenches of building sites. And, of course, actually working for the English, the very people whose imperialistic actions had caused him to leave his homeland, his relatives, his music but, not his Gaelic football.

Gaelic football has much the same rules as Australian all rules football except Australian football is more brutal because, I suppose, the Australians have a greater axe to grind.

CHAPTER 1 : GAELIC FOOTBALL

Gaelic football rules allow you to catch and hold a spherical ball with your hands and run and gain ground so long as you bounce the ball with your hands or dribble the ball with your feet. A pass can be created either by punching or kicking the ball to your teammate while running with the ball. The idea is to get the ball up the pitch so you can kick or punch the ball past the glove-wearing watchful eye of the defending goalkeeper into the back of the soccer sized goal opening net. You can gain additional points by kicking the ball directly over the area between two vertical poles.In essence, it's quite a physical game. Any self-respecting lawyer would tell you the name of the game was a misnomer and should have been called the game of assault and battery. The Irish way of encouraging team members to play well from the touchline, would mean shouting abuse towards the players.

"Sure, you'll beat that man pulling faces, John Joe!"

"Have that man out of it! – Into him."

"Ya nothing but an eejit!"

"Ya nothing but a fecking omadhaun, no better than fecking latchico! to be sure."

"Your nothing but a pure Mayo eejit."

A player's selection depended upon the county he was born in, typically games were between Mayo, Wexford, Galway and

Sligo. Shortages of players turning up and 'togging 'out to represent their county meant new teams would be formed namely St Pauls or Mitchells. Sometimes a cluster of players would be selected based on who they worked for or which public house they drank their gallons of beer. Men from Dublin would invariably make every effort to have their team called the 'Jackeens.' Every other team playing on the Glebe that linked to Dublin would be referred to by the as the 'Culchie's' because the Dublin players consider themselves more cultured than those outside the Dublin Metropolis!

Hurley is another Irish sport played on a pitch having the same symmetry as the Gaelic football game and,with the same intensity and foreboding. However, it is played with a stick having a narrow shaft and a flat end designed for hitting a small ball with a size slightly bigger but lighter than cricket ball or baseball. The game of Hurley is considered to be much faster and skilful than Gaelic and can be the result of blood injuries when the sticks are weaponised with the help of an infamous Irish temper. The game is much faster, and its genuine gravitas is its speed. Skirmishing between the competitive athletes would sometimes continue into the afternoon and then into the changing rooms. Fighting would only stop when an opponent had had a heart attack, or when somebody called the police.

The most defining moment of the afternoon happened when somebody announced; 'The pubs were open again at six-thirty' It was then off to the pub to listen to a good blast of music coming from an Irish band. It was only after a few songs would the fierce craic commence throughout the evening. During which all would be forgiven and forgotten with beer being the common dominator. Afterwards, it would be a return home to embrace the 'quare' one's greeting.

"There be no more galivanting for ya now."

"Look at ya?"

"Ya like a beast in the field – Ya banjaxed."

"Ya eejit."

CHAPTER 2 : LIVING BESIDE TINKERS

On a cold winter weekday without warning, numerous families of Irish tinkers descended on Sparkbrook in droves; they came in their vans, their caravan's, together with their dogs' horses' and trailers settling into residential roads Palmerston, Gladstone, and Grantham in particular. These particular travellers (a Lucht siuil) or Irish tinkers spoke with a peculiar Irish accent that emanated from Tipperary in the South of Ireland. Many of the locals referred to them as gypsies and pikies. Whatever you called them, it didn't matter to them because they had become indifferent to any kind of abuse, verbal or otherwise, which was the common theme throughout their oppressed, itinerate lives - it was their second nature.

Starting from day one, it was obvious they were trouble. It was only a matter of time before it became evident that they had no social or legal boundaries resulting in anti-social behaviour, illegal dog fights betting and causing disputes amongst the hardworking previously settled immigrants. Tinkers had inordinately large families, having ten plus children was the norm with plenty of room for additions, including wild dogs and scruffy looking horses. Many of them were short of digits others had too many digits, with others struggling with one arm or one leg shorter than the other, and body odours only Saint Patrick would forgive. My Dad said these particular tinkers were different from other tinkers because they didn't appear to be transient as they moved into and lived in large houses just around the corner. We wished they had not done so because the whole neighbourhood was never the same again after their arrival. They wanted to be known by their tinker surnames such as Sheridan, Holland, Gallagher, Codona, and Hearn.

Sometimes if you were running an errand for your mother down to the shops, it was common for tinkers to be loitering on the corner of Palmerston road. They would accost you and rob whatever monies you had on you. Other times they would ask you if you wanted to exchange your watch you had on your wrist for something less valuable, they possessed or had stolen earlier. They would then ask you.

"How much do ya wan for you dag?"

"Oioiiiii give ya five pounds for it next week!"

"I promise ya that on ma mother's death bed!"

"Here, spit on my hand, and that will seal it."

They could never remember anybody's first names. Leading them to labelling everybody 'Johhhhnnnn' and if you were not interested in selling 'Ya dag' they would call you 'Oinseach' and idiot and shout at you.

"Ya, nothing but a stones."

These terms of endearment eventually changed into phrases.

"Ya bollocks!" And, "Ya notting but a bollicks!!"

During the hot summer months, trouble would raise its ugly head, with tinkers being the cause of it. They would be the initiators of most fights amongst the new commonwealth immigrants. Many of these disputes would be over tiny issues. They would escalate into running clashes and violence between scores of tinkers and recently arrived commonwealth immigrants. We always had a safe panorama view from the bedroom front bay window of number 3 Palmerston Road. It made you feel as if you were viewing from a theatre balcony. These battles continued over the summer months year after year. Only when matters got out of hand would the police become involved to quell the disturbances. I remember well the first time the police were called. I witnessed one of the neighbours making a telephone call to the police station to express they're concerned over the escalating neighbours' conflicts. Subsequently, two Bobbies arrived on bicycles, which they duly parked and chained together in our front garden. They then walked up towards Grantham road only to retreat quickly, with one Bobby limping and placing his one arm on the other bobby's shoulder and his hand free to hold his helmet. His mate was sporting a black eye and a depleted ego. When they managed to return safely to their means of transport, they found both bicycles had disappeared!

After that first visit, the Sparkhill police grew savvier. Whenever the phone rang again concerning Palmerston road, the police would arrive tooled up with mechanical transportation together with the full compliments of batons. Police transportation meant large blue police vans with black cars, which were called Black Moriah's. These vehicles would be parked at the end of the Stratford road end of Palmerston road to avoid any potential damage being caused by mindless vandalism when the rioting got out of hand.The individual fistfights, name-calling and brick throwing between the varying factions continued into the late afternoon until everybody became tired and hungry and lit illegal fires. The majority of the scuffles and individual fistfights were over missing belongings or non-payment of rent. Once all the new immigrants had returned to their homes, the feuding between the Sheridans, Gallaghers, and the Docherty tribes would restart. And to make it a family affair, the wives and children joined in to make sure they didn't miss out on the night's entertainment.

There was one particular tinker who stood out from the rest

of the tribe. He had a strikingly sizeable flabby chin that hung over his collar. It was, without doubt, the ugliest sight any person would want to see in the cold light of day. He always reminded me of a bird called the pelican, which I had read about in school. He had a seedy complexion and the appearance of a man who had eaten too many scabby donkeys. It was very difficult at times not to stare at him whenever he walked past, and once you had beamed in on him, it was difficult not to keep on staring. It was a similar simulation to your mother warning you not to look at the crash on the other side of the motorway. One Saturday morning, when looking out of the bedroom window, I noticed the Pelican looking tinker with his ginger curly hair strutting with a swagger past our house and down towards the Stratford road. He walked very proudly at least two steps in front of the other tawdry members as they walked towards what you could safely assume was his wedding ceremony. They had all scrubbed up well with hair looking as if it had been brushed at least once during the previous week together with their new suede suits each with a pink coronation and, their clean white shirts lashed at the collar with a purple satin Wyatt Earp dicky bow. Unfortunately, one-part of their tunic let them down, and that was their dirty unpolished winkle pickers having ornate chrome decoration toecaps and heels. My father used to say.

"You can always tell a man's health and wealth by how much attention he pays to his shoes."

Most men never look down at their shoes and assume most people don't look at their shoes either but smart people do. That evening on the same day, I was reading a book called 2000 leagues under the sea by a man called Jules Verne when I heard a loud shrieking sound coming from the front bedroom where my sister was sowing. She shouted for me to go quickly to the room to see what she could see. From there, I could see the Pelican tinker being physically handled and dragged up Palmerston road by the very same posse of wedding guests who had escorted him down the road that morning. It eventually took the majority of the wedding contingent most of the evening to drag him past Palmerston road towards Gladstone road. He seemed very much reluctant and most determined not to go home and was making every effort not to. Dad ventured into the bedroom and saw for himself what the commotion was. He said.

"Perhaps his bride had fewer fingers he had hoped for, or he may have insulted the bride's family and, of course, like all tinkers' weddings, a fight broke out."

The last time we witnessed trouble between the varying factions was when the police were called mid-afternoon on an autumn Sunday afternoon. Fifteen minutes later, a police van pulled up at the bottom of Palmerston road, and a young police officer was forced out the blue muriahs rear doors. He slowly walked up the little hill and stopped. He then balanced himself on one leg and stretched his neck to see if there was any trouble brewing. The phone call had reported that running pitched battles were in full flow. This time, however, they appeared to have been misinformed, or possibly they thankfully arrived after the skirmish had simmered down again. This brought a sigh of relief to the young officer as he tips towed back to his waiting fraught colleagues in a blue van.

CHAPTER 2 :
THE DENTIST
WITH EXCESSIVE
TREATMENT
DISORDER

I had not visited the dentist since I was seven years of age. Like most people, you do not forget the first time you sat down in a dentist's chair. I always try not to remember the day some eejit wearing white overalls and a cheesy smile told you, 'everything was going to be perfectly alright' while he placed a rubber smelling darkish mask over my face. I remember waking up in the recovery room where I was lying down and feeling the same way E.T. must have felt when he landed on earth. I moved my head and noticed another boy lying prostrate on the next bed. He seemed to be in a more distressed state that I was. The dental nurse kept coming into the room and checking in on him. However, Mom was a very pragmatic person and decided there was nothing wrong with me, and I was acting up. I was duly pulled by the hand off the bed and told me to walk with my mother to the sweet shop where ice cream was waiting.

The next time I visited the dentist, I was thirteen years of age. I visited the dentist, not for a check-up, but because I had a raging toothache for days, The Dentist I visited was a man known in the neighbourhood as Jim Mitchel. Jim had another name which was oblivious to me. It was Jim, the 'Butcher of Sparkhill'. He gained this reputation because Jim had a propensity for filling teeth when they were perfectly good teeth. He had filled the teeth of thousands of people in the Sparkhill area with the aid of his dental surgeons' mates. All of which had studied dentistry with him at the University of Edinburgh. Jim wanted to be a doctor but failed the entrance interview so therefore tried his hand at dentistry because the hours were shorter and the money better. It didn't take him long to work out that the National health audit department was grossly incompetent. It was a period when the National health was still in its infancy and money was not valued the same way it is today. Jim, the quasi dental entrepreneur and a very greedy one at that, knew he could fill teeth without there ever being an audit of his work. This meant Jim and his colleagues made money at an exponential rate. It was only when the line of disgruntled husbands, mothers, relatives of those who had suffered or was suffering from agony for months and years, indeed, whole families eventually ended up outside the dental practice. Not to have their teeth filled once again but to fill Jim in good and proper. Why it took so long to discover for Jim's misdemeanour is still a mystery to this day. Some say it's because he was self-policing.

In contrast, in a small GP's surgery or Dental Practice with many partners, it is often the case where the existing other partners within the partnership would soon rid themselves of Jim and his antics. There was another reason being banded around at the time. And that was, he was married to a member of a famous female trio of singers called the Beverly Sisters and, many I suppose, thought that his celebrity status placed him beyond reproach. Jim was eventually, and unceremoniously, struck off by the British Dental Association for excessive treatment. And that was the end of Jim, so we thought. About ten years after his fall from grace, I read an article in the Birmingham Evening News towards to back pages. It stated that a man named James

Mitchell, who had practiced dentistry in the city a decade earlier and subsequently relocated to live in the Bahamas, had been shot dead by his attorney. I could not believe what I read at first, but it was accurate news. We all knew Jim was crooked. What we didn't realize was Jim had escalated to organized crime. Perhaps that's how and why he met the final demise. You must be rotten if your lawyer terminates your mortal coil.

News of Jim's passing continued in the local newspapers for the next few days. The Birmingham Evening Mail failed to give the full story of Jim being called the 'Butcher of Sparkhill' nor that he got struck off for excessive treatment or the fact that his wife the youngest of the Beverly sisters had divorced him. How easy it is to brush over Mr Mitchell's real misdemeanours causing untold awful pain and suffering for thousands so that he could make a quick buck.

CHAPTER 2 : PRINCE

Prince, our only pet dog, was a scruffy little mongrel. Nobody knew when he became part of the family, but he did, and thankfully he stayed for the majority of our childhood. Rumours had it that my big brother Seamus brother lassoed him and brought him back from Small Heath Park. Seamus never owned up to it so as not invoke Mom and Dad's anger. The following week after Prince descended on 3 Palmerston road, I told a friend at school that we had just adopted a mongrel dog into our family. My friend asked me if Prince was an Irish dog or an English dog. I was perplexed by this question and responded by asking him.

"Do you mean does the dog bark with an Irish accent or an English accent?"

"No, you fool!"

"An English dog eats with its owners, sleeps inside the house and, at times sleeps with his master either in the master's bed or less intimately in the master's bedroom. An English dog has a licensed vet to look after it, possibly a cute collar and lead with his name on and receives dog training together with therapy once a month."

"An Irish dog". He went on to inform me.

"Is let out without a collar and lead and is told to feck off and feed himself and don't be coming back here all hours of the night barking your testicles off."

He did have a point, Prince more or less fed himself and would wander off to see his girlfriends and returned when it suited him. If you attempted to put a collar on him, he would give you the most disgusted of looks. One day one of my older sisters dressed him up for the craic and the poor creature darted out the back door and within seconds produced a long projectile vomit.

Prince followed us everywhere during the school holidays, which included walking to and from the bus stop during school term. We took Princes' loyalty and guardianship for granted which we all very much regretted after one bad experience. One summer holiday Prince walked us to the bus stop and, instead of waiting at the bus stop, he jumped on the corporation bus heading towards a final destination in the city centre. Although Prince got off the bus with us, he seemed to lose his loyalty towards us and turned his disloyal sniffing ability to other dogs' behinds and went the canine trail instead of the human trail. None of us realized that Prince had decided to sniff his way home, and, hence, when we all finally arrived home that evening, the question was asked. 'Where is Prince?' Which brought on a silent response. We all looked at each other in anticipation of a positive response to no avail. Then, started large portions of the tears, crying, shouting, whaling, and recrimination. These reactions failed to bring poor Prince back home. He was gone forever. We all sat down and reflected on how we took poor Prince our domestic pet for granted. The poor creature who had to fend, feed, clean, cloth, guard, toilet for himself and, lastly was under strict instructions not to vastly increase the canine population of Sparkbrook was gone. Not since the Cuban missile crises had there been such domestic distress. The absence of a Prince caused untold misery in the McEvilly household. One morning when Dad was driving to work, a serendipitous meeting took place. He noticed a mangy forlorn-looking canine limping out of the city towards the general direction of Hall Green. Dad stopped his van and loaded an excitable Prince into the rear of the van and quickly returned home. Within a few seconds of my Dad returning through the front door.

"Prince is here!!" he shouted.

Upon hearing those words, we all ran downstairs in our pyjamas and gowns to see for ourselves. And, so, there he was jumping over armchairs, settees, and coffee tables entirely out of control. Then came the exchanging of canine saliva for human saliva, excessive tail wagging, frequent stroking of his back with kisses and hugs with every opportunity. I had never seen him so happy and excited, he was such a joy to watch. The welcome home celebrations lasted most of the morning, and Dad jokingly said he had not seen such celebrations since V.E. Day (day the when the war in Europe ended June 1945). That day, he explained, the whole of London's population poured on to the streets to rejoiced and partied with tables full of rationed food, amateur musicians belting out tunes from piano's, accordions and violins accompanied by the wonderful sustenance of mugs of warm English beer. After that day, we had a long discussion with our new re-evaluated pet mongrel. Prince accepted that, in this life, it was only the cat that walks alone.Therefore, Dad lectured the much-treasured canine in no uncertain terms that it would be obligatory for him to wear a collar with his name on it. Prince with his right paw resting down over his left leg, which in turn supported his chin looked upwards intently as if there had been an accident in the kitchen overnight - Thinking a dog lead was out of the question!!

During his absence younger siblings were sure they had seen Prince on the 12-inch black and white TV sitting at the side of President Kennedy barking strategic advice during those few dark days when assisting to resolve the Cuban missile crisis.

CHAPTER 2 : FARM ROAD PARK

Some weekends my brother Seamus would walk me to the park. Farm Road Park was so-called because it resembled a farm. It also had one other feature, which was a large house called Lloyd's Farm House. This particular property owned by a wealthy banking family called Lloyd, the founding members of Lloyd's banking empire.The park was within safe walking distance, and so my brother was given the task of looking after his younger brother while he has enjoyed the company of his mates. We walked through the park gate to go home with his mate Peter O'Hara when three older boys stopped us. I was six; my brother was ten and also was Peter. The biggest of the three boys asked my brother to stretch his arm out. Seamus had recognised the older boy as the neighbourhood bully. My brother knew that if he had given him his hand, he would most probably want to break it.

My brother refused to give him his hand and eventually started to cry with Peter coming out in sympathy. And of course, I began to cry because the other two were crying. Whatever I had consumed for breakfast that morning evacuated my colon and, with the assistance of gravity travelled through my gluteus maximus and deposited itself into the only spare, clean pair of underpants my mother could locate that morning. Just as it looked as if the next action to follow would be a violent action, a boy, a Carribean boy, to be precise, came around the corner on his bicycle and stopped his bike. He asked what was going on? He then looked at me and asked the others, why was I was crying. There was a silence, and I looked up at him and told him exactly what was going on. The boy looked at the bully and asked him if what I said was true. The bully told the boy to 'mind his own business' and called him a 'Nigg-Nogg'. He got off his bicycle and placed it leaning against the park gate. He then walked back and approached the bully with ugly anger on his face and hit the bully with a punch delivering it to the side of his fat face. The bully stood there as if lightening had struck him. The two other boys could not believe their eyes. Their master and commander didn't have the minerals they thought he had and, as an act of self-preservation both bolted down the road to be followed closely by my knight in armour attempting at every possible opportunity to backfill their backsides with kicks. As he returned, he winked at me and said.

"Let me know if they give you trouble again."

That act of altruism was not lost on me. I have always supported the underprivileged and the ethnic minorities because of that day at Farm Road Park. I do believe that there is always some-body who will come to your rescue in time of need.

CHAPTER 2 :
MURDER AT NR 3

Most Saturday mornings after breakfast before we headed off to see the matinee at the Piccadilly cinema, my brother and I played football at the bottom of the garden behind the garage.

On one particular Saturday, we both ran towards the bottom of the garden and on the way, mischievously opened the garden shed door causing my sister a great inconvenience when ushering the mass breakout of chickens and their chicks. I opened the double garage doors that led onto a narrow tarmac driveway. This allowed us enough football practise space to become aspiring Birmingham city or Aston Villa footballers. On this particular morning, as we approached the bottom of the garden, I knew something strange had happened. I could see through the cracks in the wooden garage doors several men in a blue type uniform looking on the ground and putting tape around a large diameter hollow telegraph pole, which we sometimes used as a goal post. There seemed to be a commotion. Some of the uniformed men were scribbling in little black handheld notebooks. One policeman was painting the pole with white emulsion-type paint. I thought this odd because why would you paint over what looked like red coloured paint which splattered on the adjacent brickwork walls and the garage doors. My brother appeared to be upset by what he saw that morning. I was too young to understand, and when I asked a question as to what was happening, he responded by telling me he would tell me later, which he never did. I found out what happened then by default through overhearing my father explaining to my mother the story that lay behind the events of that morning.

The café, which had a front entrance overlooking the main Stratford Road and rear access to the tarmac drive, we often adopted as our footy pitch. The café had become notorious in recent years for opening late hours and attracting low life customers. According to Dad, an argument broke out between two individuals within the café very late Friday night or during the early hours of the Saturday morning. Both sparing partners went out to the rear of the café to settle the argument. What one side of the two combatants did not realise was that the other side had friends waiting for him at the rear of the café. His friends decided to set about him and tie his hands around the telegraph pole. They used his torso as a punching bag for what must have been a long time because the blood splatters reached the brickwork wall five meters away. I never mentioned that day to my brother again because I knew what he saw that day upset him far more than it bothered me.

CHAPTER 2 :
CHRISTMAS
TURKEY AND THE
HOLY WATER

Christmas time in the McEvilly's household was always a time when there was an abundance of food and drink for the family, visitors and hungry close friends. Every year two brown parcels would arrive in the post a few days before Christmas Eve. Invariably, the larger of the packages would be a turkey and the other a goose. Dad would spend a great deal of time during Christmas Eve throwing water over the turkey and then plucking the feathers of both the turkey and the goose. He would also spend time burning off any stubborn feather ends, and then carried out the act of thoroughly cleaning and gutting both birds. The sight of this was always too much for me to watch. Eventually Dad would perform what appeared to be miracle. This meant retrieving two bottles from within each fowl. The bottles would be ceremonially removed using great dexterity. Each bottle had a sticker attached to the side containing Grandma McEvilly's shaky handwriting. The writing read, 'Holy water.' Dad would then sample the sacred water was pure by drinking a small sample and then place the bottles into his hidden tabernacle. I found this ritual rather strange because once it entered the tabernacle, seldom was it seen again until Dad took it out to bless himself, which of course brought about expressions of sublime bliss. Christmas liturgy repeated itself for years. It wasn't until I asked him.

"Why we were not allowed to have Christmas liturgy?Isn't it a more Christian act to share the celebration?"

He responded with a snarl on his face and thunder in his voice.

"Let yeah not be asking that shagging question again, ya little eejit, or I will eat the head off yeah."

He started to take a step towards me so as he could position himself to deliver to me a good kick up the arse, but he realised that holy water forbids such an action. Christmas day and visits to the Catholic church at St Anne's in Digbeth near the city centre was no different to any other Sunday morning service attended by the McEvilly family only, on Christmas day, the Priest would give a prolonged sermon. At least the sermon was in English unlike the mass itself, which was in Latin. I often looked around to see bored expressionless faces pretending to understand Latin, but they didn't fool me. The obligatory fast before receiving Holy Communion during mass was a real sacrifice for me. Blessing yourself with cold water, sitting on a cold hard wooden bench, kneeling for what seemed ages, getting off your knees then standing when the little altar bell rang, listening and understanding the Priest only when he delivered his sermon. I manage to understand a few words like 'Corpus Autem Christi' meaning the body of Christ.

CHAPTER 2 : ST CATHERINE'S OF SIENA CHURCH REPAIRS

One Sunday, Mom told Dad she wanted to worship at the new church time we didn't go to Anne's Christmas service. Instead, we went to St Catherine's in Lee bank on the Bristol road close to where they previously lived in the back-to-back slum property. The newly constructed Church built by a very proud west of Ireland man trading under the name Jack O'Callaghan and sons was different to other churches because it was round in shape with a dome roof. When my mother sat down on the wooden bench, I could hear her whisper to my father.

"What are all those buckets doing on the floor in various locations?"

It wasn't long into the mass when we found why the buckets were necessary. The roof was leaking in numerous places, and of course, the buckets were recipients of roof water cascading from the ceiling. My mother was so vexed she left the service in a rage saying that greedy bastard is at it again. She was fuming so badly I didn't dare to ask her why.

CHAPTER 2 : THE LODGERS

The lodgers dining room was, I was warned, most fervently out of bounds. Nonetheless, when you are an inquisitive seven-year-old, you innocently think the rules are for others. On two occasions, I sneaked into the lodger's room to have a look. The first time, I slowly turned the doorknob and opened the door to have a glimpse. There I could see lodgers eating their evening meal. An evening 'scran' of (scallion), spring unions, boiled bacon, swedes, cabbage, turnips. In the middle was a more substantial plate with potatoes (praities) and next to that was a plate of cooked ribs and (crubeen) pigs' feet on a separate plate. They then finished the evening meal, cleaned off the tables to allow them to play a game of cards. The game was called 25 and was, as far I would establish a card game familiar to the Irish. The second time I sneaked in I noticed a TV set in the corner and another armchair in the other corner. As I looked around the room two of lodgers stared at me grinningly and whispered to each other.

"Look at the little lachico!" They then asked. "Are you a Gasureen?"

They continue to engage me in conversation, asking me questions.

"Have yeah the bog in yet, young skan?" And, "How is she cutting?"

"Have yeah, the hay in again?"

"Dig it well down and throw it well back, to the maker's name."

I had no idea what they were talking about and it all seemed foreign to me. It was later explained to me by my mother that I was listening to Irish farmers dialogue. She said that 'skan' was Irish for skin and this word meant a person in that regard.

"How is she cutting?"

This was a reference to men cutting turf in the bog back in Ireland when the men were cutting a sod of turf ready to be stacked and left to dry on the ground during the summer months and then loaded into the cart and pulled by an ass back to the farm shed to be used as winter fuel.

When the game of cards started, you could hear raised voices saying.

"Hit at twenty now ya eejit" and "Why didn't you hit him at fifteen?"

"Dam and blast ya, ya old eejit!"

Eventually, the night's entertainment would be at an end and they would climb the stairs up to the attic for a good night's sleep in preparation of the following days hard manual labour.

CHAPTER 2 : SHIELDS

Three to four times a month a man would walk into the store with his hand reached outwards his eyes fixed to the floor and muttering incoherently. He was permanently clad in a tatty damaged Crombie overcoat that had never experienced the virtues of a dry cleaning. His hair was longer than it ought to have been and his beard reminder me of Black beard from the children's book called Treasure Island.He was known in and around the inner city as 'Sheilds' and nobody ever knew his real name. It was rumoured he was a relative of a well to do Irish family in the city but for whatever reason was outcast and rendered penniless from an early age. He resided in the Rowton House down in Digbeth located near the market area close to the city centre. The Rowton House was one of a chain of hostels built in London and Birmingham for the poor by Lord Monty William Lowry-Corry, 1st. Baron Rowton was also known as Monty. Born 1838 and died 1903 who was a well known philanthropist.

Irrespective of which ever ale house you were drinking in you could guarantee Sheilds would turn up over the course of the evening with his hand out looking rather pitiful and begging for money. The Irish gave him money whether it was because they wanted him to leave the premises or whether it was because they were known for having a good heart was never clear. The discerning English gave him money and were never disapproving of him. They considered him a harmless hapless begger and the acceptable face of begging because he walked to work throughout the city. The fact that he was never seen with a drink or a cigarette in his hand and known not to gamble helped his cause. This was of course not the case with some of his con-temporaries who sat around railway stations and the like wait-ing for easy money. Shields only real competition was Annie.

Annie had another name. She was called 'Pick bin' Annie and her speciality was to look in side every available council bin on every street lighting post or public bus stop. Her daily work scope encompassed a three mile distance, running along the Stratford road starting from the bottom end of Sparkhill Park all the way up to the traffic island at camp hill. Annie modus operandi meant she would carry a large bag with her so as to collect what ever she thought was valuable and fill the bag to the brim. She would then walk back to the transfer station which must have been home and then returned to repeat cycle. According to folks who remained in the area Shields stayed the course for forty years and remained at his begging duties for fifteen years longer than Annie. Perhaps, his gains were far more rewarding in terms of money. Who really knows, perhaps it wasn't about money and the real reason was an underlying problem? Annie knew her place of work would not alter from day to day and nobody would rob her because they all knew she wasn't carrying any cash.

CHAPTER 2 : MOM HAVING A BABY

One Christmas around about the time of the Cuban missile, my mother entered the hospital to have baby number eight - my youngest sister. Mom early hospitalisation was due to her reaching the grand age of forty four andthe fact she had borne seven children. Every now and again Mom would become angry with us, notably when she spoke to us in Gaelic and we responded in English with a superimposed Brummie accent. Mother reminded us of our heritage and how the British legislated the Irish language from the tongue of the indigenous folk of Ireland. She reiterated that language was not a privilege. Indeed, it was a birth right and, that you had to work hard to retain an ethnic language. The same rules applied to faith and religious beliefs.

She went on at times to remind us of how many stitches she endured during every birth. She told me that I was the only child born at home, and I did not cause her to have any stitches. She said this was because she was more relaxed when she gave birth to me in her bedroom. We did ask Mom if this was the last one as childbearing age was not an infinite resource. She responded by saying.

"Gods will, is Gods will!"

During the second day of her hospital stay, Dad informed Mom of the sad news regarding her mother's death. Grandma Nora Atkinson (Nee Flynn) had passed away peacefully back home in

Ireland. The only consolation was that she passed away quietly in her bed inside her single-storey thatched cottage where she had raised four children against all the odds. The doctor had every sympathy towards my mother plight and permitted her to return home for forty-eight hours to be with her immediate family. She walked through the front doors looking pregnant and tired. She was ranting on about the Cuban Missile crisis and how she had worked hard to raise a family and now it was in danger of it all being taken away. We didn't know if the Cuban Missile Crises upset her more than the death of her mother. I must confess even as a child, you could see by looking at the adults and the teachers at school, that the situation was grave. There was an eery silence, that kind of silence you experience when people are afrid to talk. Dad's temporary solution to a crisis, whether big or small, was always a shot of brandy to calm the nerves. However, on this occasion with Mom being at full term meant brandy was not an option. Well, it wasn't an option for Mom, but of course dad needed to be brough round!

Within a matter of a week, Mom had had baby number eight weighing in at eight pounds, and the missiles crisis in Cuba had resolved itself. The American President of the name Kennedy had brokered a deal with the then Russian Premier, Mr Khrushchev by agreeing that the USA would not invade the Island of Cuba so long as Russia did not establish missiles on the Island Cuba. All was well. Dad went back to laying a thousand bricks a day, and Mom continued working herself to the bone. Then not long after that event, we heard the dreadful news of President Kennedy assassinated in Dallas, Texas, USA. He was murdered by a lone gun called Lee Harvey Oswald. We all watched the TV scenes as it rolled out and it was gruesome to watch. Strangely everybody can remember where he or she was at that moment. I wondered genuinely why a good man who saved the world from a disastrous end got shot without apparent reason. One of my smartass cousins said he signed his death warrant when he made a speech about abolishing the Federal Reserve and the secret society like the Freemans and other secret organisations. You must remember that all power in gained through violence if, violence does not succeed then the end of a gun barrel must.

My cousin was always too clever for his own good!!

CHAPTER 2 : ASTON TV STUDIO AND THE BEATLES

One evening I read an advert in a Birmingham newspaper's evening edition describing how a ticket was able to be won by entering a competition open to everybody. To win a ticket, the entrants needed to identify a missing item from two identical photographs. They needed to describe the article and send their answers to 'Thank your lucky stars show' at Alpha TV studios in Aston Birmingham. The Studio was not far from the city, an area known for the aroma of the HP source. The factory that made the source was surrounded by back-to-back slum housing with numerous families sharing an outside toilet. What came out of that area not many years later was a young man called John Michael 'Ozzy' Osborne, who formed a heavy metal group called Black Sabbath. This band went on to achieve greatness within the world of music for decades. The band's music and popularity spread globally for decades. I have always believed that real talent comes from where you least expect it. Even from within the great unwashed, which is what one Tory Politian called the 'Working class'.

I promptly mark the newspaper picture with an X where I thought the item would be and sent it back in the post. It was a quiet struggle trying to locate an envelope moreover, a stamp that cost money. Within ten days I received a letter in the post, which came as a shock to me because nobody had ever written a letter to me. We were not a letter-writing family; Indeed, I cannot remember anybody sitting down and writing a letter. Mom always complained about the number of times we didn't visit the library to borrow books. The letter contained a ticket with instructions telling me where and what to do on a specific date which was three weeks away. I couldn't wait for that day and told everybody in the house and then concealed the ticket until the event. The date finally arrived, and I travelled to Aston with the help of two buses. The studio could be easily identifiable by the line of people queuing to enter the side door to one of the studios. Once inside the studio room, I was disappointed because it was merely a room with dark walls, a wooden three tire amphitheatre running around seventy-five per cent of the external wall perimeter. Within its centre was an area where the pop-singers and pop-groups would perform in front of those strange looking objects called TV cameras. My ticket allocation ensured that I sat in the front row on a wooden foldable chair which was most uncomfortable because rehearsals seem to take forever. What did surprise me was the number and calibre of a celebrity appearing on the production.

People who I had watched on top of pops our favourite TV Thursday night musical treat appeared within a few feet of me. We were instructed by the studio manager not to move or shout when the red light came on. I had not realised that artists mimed which meant they appeared to pretend to sing by moving their lips in front of the camera but with no sound coming out. I found this strange because, in my innocence, I believed that pop-stars sang the words in front of the TV cameras. Stars like the Tom Jones, The Searchers, Dave Clarke five, Cilla Black, Billy J Cramer, The Swinging blue jeans, The Moody Blues and finally arrived the Beatles. I was within an arm's length of the man himself, Paul McCartney. The show came to an end, and the red light switched off. What happened next came as a shock to me. Dozens of screaming hysterical teenagers leaped from their wet seats and and forced their way through the front row in order to grab a Beatle for themselves, with me in their flight path. I must admit I was never so shocked, stunned and even shaken up!!

CHAPTER 2 : MR BEST AND HIS FAMILY

The neighbour next door was also an Irish. But it must be said a more traditional English quasi family or indeed an Irish family wishing to be an English and assimilate accordingly. That meant only having one child, never going to church, listening to the Queen's speech on Christmas day and letting the neighbours know when they were about to brew a pot of tea. It was always possible to known when it was tea time next door because you could hear the kettle whistle too many time a day

The kitchen was at the back end of the house, which was a hallway and dining room distance from the living room, which meant they could not hear the whistling for ten to fifteen minutes at a time. This was most annoying if you were playing in the garden.Now and again.

Phyliss thought she would take pity on me and ask me in to play with her son Patrick. This act of kindness initially made me happy. However, there was an ulterior motive. Her spoilt brat of a son had nobody to play with besides me. I suppose he was selfish at his best and found it challenging to share with others of his age. It was during that time we played together that I realised it wasn't his fault that the mother decided to be selfish and only have one child. Her actions caused a great deal of unhappiness for those materially concerned. Phyllis was always preening her feathers, which meant putting cream on her face or powdering her nose. When going out shopping, she would invariably put her stocking on in front of the TV, which meant she would pull up her skirt and somehow clip the top end of her stocking to some restraining device called 'Suspenders'. Sometimes she would sit down and cross her legs to put her stocking on while watching the 12-inch black and white TV causing her to reposition her legs, which exposed parts of a woman's anatomy I had never seen before. I would have looked away, but I found the situation titillating but was too young to know why it was titillating.

One evening when I was playing in the house next door with Patrick, I heard a knocking coming from the front door. The door-knocking was unusual because, as far as I could remember, nobody ever visited except for Phyllis' mother who, just happened, to live next door. When Hugh opened the door, a bespectacled tall Jamaican man appeared standing in the rain. There was a short discussion, and the man entered into the hallway placed his umbrella into the lower rail of the hat stand, took off his raincoat and trilby hat and put both on the upper track of the hat stand. He then proceeded to follow Hugh to the living room, and we all sat down. During the evening, Mr Best impressed all those listening to him that he was a confident man with a vision for the future and knew what he wanted. Mr Best with his gold cap filling and expensive spectacles had a confident demeanour in terms of education and confidence. He said the UK government would not accept his Jamaica qualifications as a trained and qualified technician. Therefore, he needed to seek employment as a mechanic. He went on to explain that he was a Jamaican citizen and came from Kingston the Capital of Jamaica. I don't think anybody knew where Jamaica was on the map and Kingston was out of the question. Mr Best was a very much respectable gentleman who spoke the Queens English an awful lot better than we did and he spoke with an educated, refined accent. He believed he and his family had a better future living in the United Kingdom if they become a subject of Her Majesty the Queen. Towards the end of the meeting, it dawned on me that Mr Best had come to discuss the purchase of the house and it eventually transpired that Mr Best relative was in the process of buying Phyllis' mother's home next door. The sale of both properties went through without a sale board. Both her and her mother decided to sell their properties and escape under the darkness of the night. Perhaps they thought the area was on the decline or they didn't like living in an area where commonwealth immigrants settled in large numbers or even worse, living next door to a large, noisy Irish family that wanted to party now and again.

A few weeks later the Best family moved in next door. I noticed a girl playing in next-door back garden. So, I reached over the fence and talked to talk to her. She happened to be a pleasant well-dressed and well-spoken young girl. After asking her loads of questions, I ran into our kitchen where my mother was, as usual, preparing food for everybody. I said in a very excitable voice.

"Our posh neighbours were black and they only had one child in the family."

My mother snapped back.

"You cannot refer to the neighbours as black people. They should be called Caribbean people and they have travelled a long way to live next to us. They have sacrificed their climate, friendships and family ties to make a better life for themselves in this great country so, show them courtesy and respect at all times!"

I asked if they were related to the darkies shown on the tooth-paste boxes available to buy on the new supermarket shelves on the Stratford road. My mother looked at me in a puzzled way and asked me if I had any inkling towards reading a book or finishing my homework.

Soon after that incident, my father decided to change his mode of transport from a small van to saloon car called a Ford Cortina. The change in vehicles came as a great shock to us all because Dad always found his van useful to transport stuff around from one site to the next. However, we all appreciated the comfort of a car over a van. About thirteen months after taking ownership of the vehicle, the engine started to miss fire. According to the quasi experts, the engine was burning oil, which is not a good sign. So, Dad decided to ask for some quotes from the local repair garages. To his amazement, all the repair quotes were well above his anticipated budget; Worse still, this unforeseen additional expenditure would have a severe impact on his beer budget. It was then I decided to let Dad in on a little secret. The secret was that Mr Best was a skilled motor mechanic and would be more than pleased to have a look under the bonnet. It was not long after my revelation that Mr Best poked his head under the hood and gave Dad the bad news. The second and third piston rings had disintegrated for no apparent reason. But as they say, every cloud has a silver lining, and as such Mr Best said he could repair the engine at a fraction of the cost a garage would charge.

CHAPTER 2 : THE BIG FIGHT AT THE HARP

One summer afternoon, Mom was at the kitchen sink peeling potatoes for the Sunday roast when I heard a knock coming from the front door. I ran downstairs and opened the door. Stood, there was my Mom's best friend. She asked me if I knew if my mother was at home I answered, yes. Mom shouted from the kitchen to come in. The woman walked down the short corridor, and before she could enter the kitchen, she started saying there was going to be an awful big fight at the Harp dance hall and the men were all getting worked up for the skirmish.

My mother looked worried she dried her hands and took off her pinner, put on her coat and walked very quickly out the door with me trailing beside her. The Harp was an Irish dance hall with a bar that opened midday on the weekends. It was not as large as the dance hall in the city entre call the Shamrock but it was just as famous principally for the Irish within a three to four-mile radius of the Sparkbrook area. We walked from Palmerston road to Walldorf road, which should have taken approximately five minutes, but Mom was near to running and with me trailing we got there in three minutes. As we approach the Harp, you could hear and see hundreds of people standing on the pavement looking on at several men fighting each other. You could listen to men with Dublin accents shouting.

"Come over here now, yeah culshie bastards, come over here, and we'll put manners on yeah once and for all yeah, fecking bogtrotters."

Some of the Dublin men turned their backs on the men from the west and pulled their trousers and underpants down shouting.

"Pog mo thoin…kiss my arse."

Men on the other side of the road, shouted back with West of Ireland accents in reply.

"Yeah narrow back work-shy eejits, sure ya, good for nothing Nancy boys, fecking plebs."

The Dublin accents were different. Men would cry 'Jaysus' instead of Jesus and, they would always be 'Blem't' for everything instead of blamed. The Dublin city men wore clothing in keeping with Englishman, as they consider themselves more in tune with the more sophisticated folk living in a British city. Unlike the West of Ireland, men who did not have any idea how to dress appropriately. The West of Ireland men stood next to this huge giant of a man with the appearance of Hercules. He must have been twenty-five stone. He stood there laughing and grinning with a big red face bending down and pulling faces towards the Dublin men on the other side of the road. Each Dubliner took in turns to hop step and jump towards him attempting in mid-air to hit him with their fists. Or, whatever they could within the short time allowed before the giant of a man caught them with one hand by the throat and with the other hand grabed them by their wives wedding present. You could hear screeching and howling from the half-drunk baying spectators on either side of the road. As the individual fighting progressed you could hear voices shouting.

"Give it to him John Joe!"

"Give him plenty of the leather!" – "Array's! Don't spare the leather!"

"Whatever yeah do don't let any of those latchico's get up off the floor!"

"If they get up, they will beat yeah!"

"Don't let that Jackeen, that dub, get the better of us otherwise, we will never hear the end of it"

Twenty minutes into the battle, I could hear glasses and beer bottles shattering on the road and could see missiles flying in the air. I heard one of the adults shouting be careful lads the Dublin boys have scaena (Knifes) It was at this point I became afraid of getting hurt. I had become separated from my mother and started looking for her in the general direction of home - out of harm's way. My mother had been searching for Dad to ensure that he was safe and not caught up in the afternoon's entertainment. Dad, with a few of his drinking companions, had been watching the brawl from a distance out of harm's way.

It was only a matter of time you could hear the sound of Police sirens and bells becoming louder and louder. Suddenly many of those men throwing punches and kicking each other in the street could be observed running at break neck pace down the Waldorf road towards the BSA with police and their sniffer's dogs following closely behind their entrails.

The harp club did have its advantages in so far, we could earn extra money stacking shelves behind the bar. This idea came from Mr O'Rourke's son, who was a couple of years older than I was. He talked to the manager who just happened to rent one of Mr O'Rourke's houses. So, every Saturday and or Sunday afternoon, we were sent to stack the shelves behind the bar. One Saturday afternoon the manager asked if one of us would like to come and help in the cloakroom on the forthcoming Saturday night because a famous singer was going to appear at the Venue. He said her name was Dusty Springfield and she had a lot of top twenty hits - whatever that meant. The manager said he only wanted Mr O'Rourke son to work in the cloakroom because, he said, I was too young. Of course, I was having none of that, so, we both arranged that I would enter the dance venue surreptitiously. When Saturday night arrived, all went to plan, and I was in the cloakroom instead of reading a book in bed. The famous singer decided to use the room next to the cloakroom to change her travelling gear into her stage dress. She decided it was far more appropriate because she had noticed that there were gaps in the changes room door and men being men, were not to be trusted to behave themselves.

When Dusty Springfield arrived, she disappeared to the changing room next to the cloakroom and was in there for ages. She came out cladded in her stage dress looking a million dollars, which turn me into smitten state. My wide eye expression caught her attention, which persuaded her to talk to me. I was shocked and stunned that she would want to speak to a mere mortal like me, but she was very laid back and down to earth. She told me her real name was Mary O'Brien from Dublin city, and she was in the original singing group called the Springfield's. She asked what a young fellow like me was doing in a cloakroom so late at night. If only she knew. My only comment or observation was I could not see into her eyes correctly or as much as I would like to because she wore some heavy black make up around her eyes. I learned later it was called mascara.

The following afternoon we were back stacking empty shelves. I remembered what Mr O'Rourke told me about finding money on the floor after a fight. I searched with an eagle eye and managed to find one five-pound note under a table and a ten-pound note behind the bar. I told Mr O' Rourke that I found a one-pound note on the floor near the toilet. That was my first practical lesson on trickle-down economics.

CHAPTER 2 : THE JOY OF JUNIOR SCHOOL

I was five years of age when I attended my first day at school and like any first day at school for a child of my generation. You could call it my second baptism. The first one, I knew very little of but, the second baptism felt like a baptism of fire – It's the very day many people reckon they can still remember as vividly daunting. My mother insisted on all of us attending the Catholic junior school in Yardley Wood because it had an excellent reputation for discipline, education standards and religious instruction. She had enquired into the schools much closer, but the majority of them failed to achieve the numbers when obtaining a place at grammar school. Moreover, many of her friends had sent their children to attend that school.Travelling to school meant going on a bus with a number 13 on the front and back heading out of the city centre towards the outer suburbs. Every morning she would order us to stand in line to receive the issuing of two plastic bus tokens. I was lucky because my elder sister of two years, who also attended the same school, would watch over me for the first two days. After that, I was on my own and left to my own devices.

The number 13 bus stop was only 100 yards from our front door. It was the only bus that travelled from our address directly to the gates outside the school gate, which took around 30 to 40 minutes on average. Children from the inner-city locations namely Camp hill and Digbeth would be on the bus waiting to start up a conversation on the previous evening's events.

The bus was always a standard colour of cream and Royal blue, which you entered at the rear and the bus conductor would stand and wait with a metal ticket machine for everybody to embark. When it was time, he would press the circular button located above his head with either his finger or his thumb.

By the time the school bus reached Sparkbrook, it would have collected several pupils from previous inner-city stops. One of my classmates, called Carol, would already be seated on the bus. Carol, with her ginger hair, was naturally bubbly and intelligent and was not the type of girl who suffered fools easily. Further, into the journey, the bus would reach Wake Green road, which was an area on the periphery of Moseley. There a boy called Phillip jumped on the bus. Neither Carol nor I liked this boy because he had a false perceived opinion of himself, spoke with his pseudo posh accent, which he thought entitled him to talk down to his classmates. On more than one occasion he would overstep the mark and issue one insult too many which in turn brought on Carols' wrath. Carol would without warning take off her school bag hanging from her shoulder and then her school blazer and give him several straights shots into his face in rapid succession. The rapidity of the shots shocked and stunned him into standing still. It was a magnificent sight to see watching the underprivileged punishing the over-privileged son of a middle-class Irish doctor. So much was it a pleasure to see I would tell Carol while spectating from the rear.

"Give it to him again Carol, give it to him again."

Of course, the repeat performance was even better. No matter how many times this situation repeated itself, the little spoilt brat would continue to receive the same punishment for the same social miss demeanour. The school had many pupils like Phillip, whose parents were either a teacher, had wealth or, had a profession. It wasn't difficult as a child to identify those who received special treatment from the teacher or received all-round betterment.One school day afternoon when I was standing at the unusual bus stop waiting for the nr 13 bus to take me home the spoilt brat Philip hit me in the face without any warning. The punch hurt because I wasn't expecting it. I put my school bag down on the ground and took off my school blazer. After that, a junior fistfight ensued. It went on for a short while before Phillip started crying because he realised that the boy from Sparkbrook was a better boxer than the boy from Moseley.

Meanwhile, other pupils became spectators and surrounded us. Phillip then decided to stop boxing and started talking to other pupils. I thought the fight was over and like a fool turned my back and stepped towards my jacket and bag lying on the ground only to be struck by an uppercut punch from the rear. This punch was so devastating it damaged the front teeth from my upper and lower jaws, resulting in the tops of six teeth losing their enamel. They remain with me to this day. It was a lesson to be learned; never turn your back on anybody in a fight. He confessed later that the idea to do it came from a friend who I know to this day. Well, I jumped on the nr 13 bus and sat in a seat on the top deck of a crowded bus and cried all the way home. Not one adult asked me why I was crying for so long and uncontrollably. I got home and shouted from the hallway into the kitchen, telling my mother that, I was going to the park but, instead, I went upstairs like a boxer in the corner well beaten but ready to fight another day.

CHAPTER 2 :
ATTENDING SPEECH
THERAPY

At the grand age of six or seven, it was decided by the experts that I would need to attend a particular speech training school regularly. It was explained to me by my older siblings 'nobody could understand what I was saying.' I was required to attend an initial interview. The speech therapy school situated at the end of what seemed to be a long road called George Road in Edgbaston. It took two bus journeys to travel there and a long walk down to the end of George road. I remember well the first interview. The therapist asked me to name all the objects she showed to me on every card she held up. There was one I failed on; it was a knitting thimble. I suppose I should have recognised one but, in mitigation, my mother never had time to knit or sow anything she was always too busy looking after all of us including the lodgers.

In practice, this arrangement more or less ruined my junior school my education. It then became the norm for me to spent my time travelling to school for approximately an hour and a half. I would then go back to Sparkbrook to jump on another bus numbered eight. This bus took me to Edgbaston five ways. Once I got off the bus and then walk a distance down George road. I would attend speech therapy, which lasted around one hour. Once finished, I would walk up George road and jump on the number thirteen bus on the return journey. By the time the bus reached Stoney lane again, it was mid-afternoon, and therefore too late to returned to school. This meant I was abscent from school for two to three days a week.

I would spend hours travelling to and from the therapist. I was given no reading book to read during my long bus rides which meant my early education and development suffered. No questions asked about my safety or whether I had had my lunch by any of the teachers. I was only ever accompanied once during the years to and from George Road speech therapy school. The second time I attended the speech school, they gave me a framed rectangular wooden template having different shaped holes. They then gave me two pegs, one having an oblong shape the other a square shape. The tutor asked me to put the correct shaped pegs into the correct holes through the timber template. When I heard this request, it brought the inner anger from within me, and I thought Jesus! Is this a speech therapy session, or a Noddy and Big ears show.

I then had a cathartic moment and threw the stuff to the other side of the room. The therapist could see I was upset and elected not to confront the issue but to continue with the next part of the lesson. That afternoon I stole a little metal taxi from the toy box and brought it home with me. I confessed to the priest during my next confession. He asked me to say five our Fathers and ten Hail Mary's as an act of penance. I suppose cynics might reflect that I was lucky to get away with just that. I believe the experience of having to travel to George road school on my own every day during those early years was a test on my early character, which enabled me to take on challenges and overcome circumstances where others would shy away.

CHAPTER 2 : MRS MEEHAN

When riding the bus to school every morning, I noticed that there would always be a grey-haired stern-looking woman sitting in the same seat every school day morning. The seat in the front of the bus overlooked the huge engine bonnet. She sat there with her handbag perched on her lap, taking full advantage of the panoramic view, which ensured she missed very little. Every morning she appeared stoic and expressionless as she donned a heavily white powered and rouge face, which masqueraded an underlying fascia that concealed more wrinkles than any living elephant had on its backside.

We always sat on a seat as far as it was possible away from her. We believe that this woman was, the devil reincarnated. We prayed every morning for a miracle, hoping she might have a personality transplant that would help her show some kindness towards her pupils. Undoubtedly, this was never going to happen because she had no friends, no pets or favourites. She simply hated everybody she encountered. Her name was Mrs Meehan, and she originally reigned from the Kingdom of Dublin. Where within Dublin nobody ever knew but it must have been a dark, and dank place just like her personality. She was the teacher who taught Class 8. Hers was the last class at the end of the corridor, and you qualified to enter that class by reaching ten years of age by a certain date. It was the last class at primary school. In her class, you were to be prepared for transition and sometimes harshness of secondary school. Therefore, the instilling of discipline during the last year of the primary was a pivotal part of the school curriculum. And my God, she loved the discipline and bullying of young children. She issued you fifty lines if you talked in class or dropped a pencil and broke its graphite. She would call you out in front of the class she would slap you if you did something wrong or make you stand in the corner and with a hat on your head with a big D on the front of it denoting that you were a dunce or as she would say it a 'duffer.'

As we grew older and closer to qualifying to enter Mrs Meehan's class, the more terrified, we became. I told my Mom one day about the antics of Mrs Meehan, and she didn't say much, but later I heard both Mom and Dad having a conversation about here while eavesdropping. Dad said, as I managed to strain my ear to its decibel receiving ability.

"Oh! She is a typical snob, an Irish snob the worst one of all, an Irish woman with an empty head."

There was one boy in my class, and his name was Jimmy Prestige, and his family lived in the local council estate. Jimmy was a little shorter than me and had that air about that told you he didn't care much for authority or anybody who hid behind it to achieve his or her own ulterior goals. One morning Mrs Meehan slapped Jimmy very hard on the back of his hand and said to him in front of the class that he was the most stupid boy she had had the misfortune to teach. As the tear full Jimmy came walking back to ink welled desk, we both shared, he turned around and called out to her.

"Fucking bitch."

We all froze with fear and looked straight ahead with amazement. Mrs Meehan said nothing and, continued as if nothing had happened. It was soon after that little incident she started on about reading the correct papers, particularly those papers issued on Sunday.

"Under any circumstances you are not to read Sunday newspapers unless it had Catholic Herald printed on top of the front page or, indeed papers of that nature."

"Comics were acceptable, providing our parents had purchased them."

Somehow her little rambling epistle didn't seem to work on the unconvertable, and the slapping of Jimmy Prestige episode repeated, and as you would expect, it achieved the same result. This time Jimmy's verbal tirade was louder and was extended to add in a few more expletives. Again, Mrs Meehan remained stoic. After the second confrontation, things seem to settle down. Two weeks had passed, and we were all in Mrs Meehan's class reading, and she called me out to the front of the class and shouted at me for getting a simple addition wrong on my maths exam. She said I was stupid and anybody coming from Sparkbrook was stupid. She then grabbed my hand to slap it hard on the back. I tried to pull it away because she was a tall, strong woman and her slaps hurt a lot.

As she was trying to hit me, she was saying, that I was a stupid young boy because I needed speech therapy and nobody else needed to have those lessons. I lost it once I heard that coming out of her mouth and somehow managed to grab the classroom door keys that she had placed on top of her desk and ran towards the door shouting for Jimmy to come and, called Mrs Meehan a dirty old bitch. I opened the door and closed it behind me quickly. Had I waited for a second longer for Jimmy, the old trout would have been able to physically opened the door before I could lock it properly. She started shouting.

"Come back here, Martin McEvilly, opened this door now, or I will call your mother and father, and they will need to come to the school to put manners on you."

Behind Mrs Meehan stood Jimmy Prestige shouting.

"Don't open the door Martin, don't open the door, she has a stick in her hand and she wants to beat you with it."

It was hard work trying to keep the door closed and attempting to lock it with a key. I had one knee pressing against the door reveal and one hand on the door most of the time. The remainder of the other time, I was making every effort to lock the door. The last bellow I heard was Mrs Meehan's voice.

"You will regret this young man as long as you live!"

While she was saying a few threatening words, I could hear some of the girls in the classroom crying and sobbing and wanting their mommies. I shouted at Mrs Meehan through the door saying.

"My Dad said you're an empty-headed Irish snob and that's the reason you can't get a boyfriend. You're too strict!"

Unlike the girls, the boys were silent, perhaps they were too afraid to express any happiness that one of them had escaped the misery of Catholicism for a short period. Eventually, after a hell of a struggle, I manage to turn the key and lock the door. I ran down the stairs to the ground floor and stood standing there, thinking about my next move. I could hear the girls screaming in the classroom and, Mrs Meehan's shouting through the door keyhole thinking I was still standing behind it. Because the classroom was at the end of the corridor, nobody could hear the screams and of course Mrs Meehan's high octaves of rage and frustration. I thought to myself that the shortest way home was to run past the classrooms 7,6,5,4. This would inevitably lead me to pass Mr O' Sullivan's office and the escape from Mrs Meehan's would have been short-lived because Mr O' Sullivan's office was located to stop this sort of thing – Well, so I thought so anyhow. So, plan B escape route meant running around the toilets up the concrete access ramp which gave me access on to the Trittiford Road. Doing this meant I needed to pass the Classroom 8 where all the miserable captives were caged. So, be it I did! I ran up the hill and noticed all the boys were staring through the classroom windows with their flat noses. Some of them you could hear were shouting.

"Run Martin, run away as fast as you can and get away from here."

Other boys could not believe that this was happening and looked lost.

I decided to run as fast I could up the hill of Trittiford road until I became so out of breath I stop with exhaustion. In front of me was Billesley Common, which was a common open area for schools to use as football pitches and the like. I spent some time watching older schoolboys playing football and played on the swings for a while. I then decided to walk towards home using the bus route as a compass. Walking past Swan Hurst Park, I stopped and jumped on some more swings and went a little dizzy on the roundabout. I eventually managed to return home mid-afternoon to be greeted by my mother. She asked.

"What are you doing home so early?" I told her "I didn't feel that well!"

"That's strange, nobody contacted me from school."

I was tired due to all the walking and playground activities and thought it wise to go to bed and count my blessings that Mom was oblivious to the truth regarding my previous morning's antics. That evening when I was half asleep in my bed, I could hear adults talking in the lounge room. They sounded like police officers telling my parents that they had scoured half of south Birmingham chasing reported sittings of me on the run – they were not happy. However, they were delighted to hear no harm had come out of my delinquency. They were invited to go and see the headmaster the following day for an adult conversation about me, which thankfully meant I didn't need to see that old bitch Mrs Meehan for another day at least. Mom was glad nothing came of it and Dad stated.

"Well, I never thought he was that spunky!"

I went to school the following day, and everybody acted as if nothing happened. Soon after that, an orange coloured mock exam papers called the eleven plus landed on my desk. I must admit the vast majority of the paper was incomprehensible to me as I had spent the majority of my time of time travelling to speech therapy school in Edgbaston and then back home. I asked my schoolmate and bus travelling companion Carol, what it all meant, and she seems to have a good idea of what was going on.

CHAPTER 2 : THE CASE OF THE MISSING HUSBAND

Mr and Mrs O'Brien were an Irish couple that lived about fifteen houses further up on Palmerston Road. They seemed to be a happy couple but had no children to speak of, which was a wretch because ironically, the McEvilly's believed in more the merrier. Mrs O'Brien called in to talk with Mom regularly, notably when running out of the necessaries like milk, butter and sugar. Mom always with her good Irish heart gave to Mrs O'Brian without hesitation whatever she needed even though the grocery shop was only seventy yards around the corner. I suppose she liked her company and of course they would talk about the old country and how life was so much slower, happier and indeed less complicated. They would chatter for ages about their respective parents as if they were still alive. Mr O'Brien would see Dad in the local pubs from time to time and they would buy each other a pint and would talk about the Dublin Gaelic football team and the price of heifers in Mayo cattle markets.

Mom and Mrs O'Brien were talking in the kitchen when she received a telephone call from Ireland, and it was terrible news. Sadly, her younger brother Wille Jo had died at the breakfast table in front of his four young children. Willie Jo had been suffering from a goitre for several months but did not have the money to see a doctor. Like most men, he never complained and continued to work on to support his family commitment.

He was unable to see the Doctor, he didn't appreciate the danger of having an untreated ailment like a goitre. My mother needed to go back and bury him and sort out family matters and then returned. It was on another occasion when both Mom and Mrs O'Brien were talking in the kitchen to each other, and I over-heard Mrs O'Brien talking to her about an English family called Houghtons that lived up in Gladstone road. They were infam-ous within the immediate neighbourhood because of its size. Seventeen children in total, some you never saw or heard of, and some were never out of trouble. She relayed to Mom that one of Mrs Houghton's daughters went to the fish and chip shop last Friday to buy fish chips for the whole family. Once the Cypriot fish and chips shop owner completed the order, wrapped every-thing up and placed it in several carrier bags. She told him that her Mom would pay him on Friday. The owner let out a shrill in anger and shouted.

"But...It's Friday today!!!"

After a minute, or so he simmered down

"I will talk to your mother later."

There seemed to be a greater understanding of hardship those days, particularly amongst immigrants after the war. Maybe many of them still remember the ration books or perhaps were just happy to have survived the war.

A month after Mrs O'Brien told my mother about the fish and chip shop tale, I was walking home from Farm Road Park and noticed that there was a police car parked outside the O'Brien home. I ran home quickly and told my mother. She was in the kitchen preparing the evening meal when I told her. She took off her pinner and walked quickly up the street. By the time my mother reached the O'Brien's, the police car was starting to pull away. Mom knocked on the green front door and a rather dis-traught Mrs O Brien answered. She was crying and immediately gave my mother a close embrace. Mom turned and gestured for me to go home. She returned home later, and I heard her talking to Dad. Mr O'Brien has gone missing for two days, and Mrs O'Brien had no idea where he could be. She had tried all the old friends' and relatives in Ireland & England, workmates and hospitals.

All avenues had been exhausted. It was on the news within a week that a certain gentleman from the Irish Republic but now living in the Sparkbrook Area had gone missing without cause. After two weeks, there was still no news and Mom spent a great deal of time comforting Mrs. O'Brien. Then one Monday morning two cars arrived carrying police officers, some in police uniforms and others were in plain clothes. They all entered the premises where the O'Brien's lived and were in there for some time. They then came out with cardboard boxes full of what looked like somebody's personal belongings. The following day they collected Mrs O'Brien and drove her to the police station. She was there for three hours and then returned but did not want to talk to anybody. Then a week later two blue coloured vans with trailers carrying digging tools and equipment arrived and parked immediately outside the O'Brien premises.

Men wearing white overalls got out and erected a tent to the front of the house and then starting digging up the rear garden undercover of a white tarpaulin and lights. We could hear the sound of a generator and could see then working at night under floodlights. The workmen were there for up to two weeks and then left. Two days after that they came for Mrs O'Brien and took her to the police station for more questioning only this time, she was in the police station with her solicitor for two days. She did not appear in public for a whole week. She came to our house for a visit us to borrow some sugar and milk because of the closed shops and said very little. The day after she returned to talk to Mom and said she had the worst time of her life because she was interrogated for 48 hours nonstop and accused of killing her husband and deposing of the body somewhere. She told them that it was rubbish, and they had no evidence to support their claim or accusation.

"Without a body; there is no crime."

"Jesus! why did he walk out of the marriage without having the common decency to tell his wife beforehand"

It seems that the message must have got home because they did not continue with their enquiries. Though Mrs O'Brien looked shaken and dishevelled, she continued with her life and ignored all the unwelcomed looks, strange phone calls and, name-calling by the children in the street.

Three years passed by and the saga of the missing Mr O'Brien was absent from the minds of most inhabitants of Palmerston road. Then one Monday morning, Mrs O'Brien decided to visit her GP. She felt depressed and was generally feeling unwell and run down after all that had happened. What she wanted was somebody to confide all her anxieties and, who better to tell but your local GP. It was a surprised for her to discover her old doctor who had treated her for years had taken early retirement. The new doctor was young and eager who went on to say that her medical records told him she rarely visited the doctor. He had worked at the surgery before as a locum and would continue to assume the duties of the previous GP.

He then asked.

"How is your husband?" Mrs O'Brien stared at the doctor with steely cold blue eyes and asked.

"What do you mean, Doctor? How is my husband?" The doctor looked at her and knew instantly that a raw nerve was touched.

"Yes." he said.

"Mrs O'Brien, your husband, if I remember correctly, came to see me as he said he was feeling tired so after examining him I referred him to an experienced heart specialist in a major teaching hospital in London"

"His heart was in a fragile condition, Mrs O'Brien."

"The outer walls of his heart had become paper thin caused by years of heavy smoking and drinking."

Mrs O'Brien started to look morose, and so the doctor asked her to sit on a chair. She told the doctor about the events of the last three years. The doctor listened with a sympathetic ear.

"Mrs O'Brien, your husband must have been a good and caring husband wishing you no distress. It is such a shame your husband did not come to see me earlier. He would have had a better chance of survival?"

Mrs O'Brien made several telephone enquiries to the London metropolitan police inquiring into her husband's disappearance. After waiting for around a week, she received a telephone from a police officer.

"He was from the Railways police department at Euston Station."

He asked Mrs O'Brien.

"If she could come to London to view the personal belongings of a gentleman who suddenly died of a heart attack on Euston Station platform one on the same day Mrs O'Brien said her husband disappeared."

The policeman told her. "This might give you closure and relieve you of the misery of not knowing, and finally put an end to the search for her husband?"

She told my mother what the police officer had asked of her, and my Dad drove her to New Street Railway station. That afternoon she identified the clothes lying in a cardboard lost property box as that of her husbands who had been missing for three years prior. When she returned to Birmingham, she told my parents that it was a relief to have closure to the long-running saga.

CHAPTER 2 : ERIC

Sometime during the summer school holidays between returning from our holiday in Ireland and going back to primary school, we noticed a young black boy and his family had moved into a terraced house seven doors up from ours. They were from the Caribbean and were the second black family to move into a house in Palmerston road. We were glad he was a boy because the Best family next door only had a daughter and her Mom was a little snobby and would not allow her to mix with ruffians like us next door.

Eric was tall, bordering on being lean, athletic and good looking and made friends sooner than later. He spoke rapidly, and better English than we did in terms of grammar which, let face wasn't tricky. His noticeable defect was a turned eye and, for this reason, we all felt sorry for him and found it easy to befriend him. Feeling sorry for him, I decided I wanted to help him and ask him if he wanted to play sports at Farm Road Park with the other lads in the neighbourhood. We started on the swings and mucking around on the slides seeing if we could slide to the end of the horizontal slide and fall off. We then noticed two teams of boys wearing white flannels and playing cricket in the flat-sanded open areas most children used for playing football. They appeared to be of Indian and Pakistani background. It was unusual for inner city boys to wear white flannels because of the expense. Eric and I looked at each other and through envious eyes and with spontaneity said to each other. 'Do you think they would they allow us to play with them?' I was so impressed with both teams of boys wearing mostly white Flannels. The same white flannels I witnessed international cricketers wore whenever I watched cricket at the Edgbaston cricket ground with my brother.

The game of cricket is primarily an English game played in schools during the summer months. The more affluent you are, the more likely you are going to play cricket wearing full flannels. The complete cricket set is expensive in comparison to other sports. In football, you need a ball, boots and a kit. After all, said and done, cricket is the preserve of the middle classes as is rugby. Unfortunately, the British have a weaponised sport to divide the classes. You only need to count how many privately educated young men play rugby and how many young men who attended secondary modern school play football.

Eric had the more approachable voice, so we decided he would ask them for a game. They looked at both of us inquisitively and looked at each other and then said 'Yes'

"Where do you play in the outfield?" they asked

Eric said he preferred to play in the same position as his West Indian cricketing hero Garfield Sobers the all-rounder and left-arm fast-medium bowler.

I told them I wanted to be Jeffrey Boycott. They gave me a peculiar look when I mentioned Boycott because he was quite a controversial, young Yorkshire batsman with strong views at that time.

The game restarted with us included. After about fifteen minutes they decided to allow Eric to bat, which was good to watch because the bowling was aggressive and he was a natural batsman scoring twenty runs. Eventually, he was caught at second slip. They then asked me to bat, and so I stood at the crease and lined my bat with the crease and looked around at the outer field waiting for the first ball. It seemed to take ages, and I asked fielding cricketers at first and second slip.

"When is he going to bowl the ball?"

A few seconds later, a loud, deep voice said. "He has already bowled two balls you prat."

As you can imagine, it wasn't long after that little exchange that I started walking back to the quasi pavilion next to the swings.

A week after my debacle of a cricket performance in front of all my commonwealth cousins my mother informed me that, Mrs Price, the lady at number twelve Palmerston road was going to throw an afternoon party for younger and older children's. Specifically, those children who lived on the road. This party was happening on Saturday afternoon. I didn't mind it being on a Saturday afternoon so long as I could hear the football results and be allowed to buy the pink coloured Argus Sports results paper that contained all the sporting results. We were all invited, but, in reality, only I would attend because the other siblings would always be doing other activities. I seem to remember number twelve had a commodious lounge, which was the venue for other previous parties.

I told Eric about the party, and he seemed delighted to come along, as it would be his first party after leaving his homeland in the Caribbean. We arrived all spruced up and ready to consume as many soft drinks and sandwiches as our empty stomachs would allow. When we entered the big room, I felt as if we were in Aladdin's cave because all the sweets you could imagine were on foldable table in the corner. In the other corner, there was another table with home-baked cakes, scones, birthday cakes, crisps bottles of Tizer, Tango, Fanta, Vimto, Red Cola, Lucozade, cans of Coca-Cola, and Pepsi.

For a good thirty minutes we filled our faces with food and poured as much Tizer and Coca-Cola down our throats. We then all decided to rest like a pride of lions after a huge feast of Antelope. Mrs Price decided then it might be a good idea to play her new plastic '7-inch' 45 RPM record. On came Frank Sinatra 'Come Fly with me'. Then, came Dean Martin singing 'Everybody loves somebody' but nobody raised their backsides off the wooden chairs that followed the perimeter of the room. After that some rock music was played and everybody jumped up and started dancing except for Eric. I was wondering why Eric would not dance with us, maybe perhaps, it was his turned eye or that he was the only non-white person in the room. I said nothing because he might be upset and I figured it best not to say anything when folk are upset as it only aggravates the situation. Within a few minutes of noticing Eric's dilemma, Mrs Price played another record, and it was dance music by an American called Chubby Checker, and the dance was called the twist. I heard the music before but didn't take too much noticed of it until Eric jumped out of his seat and started performing the 'Twist'. Eric danced in a way that was so different from any other person I had seen dance before. All the mothers and girls older than us were mesmerised by Eric's ability to dance without sudden movements with his hands and feet his whole body moved in a reggae synchronised harmonisation. Every female in the room, whether married or single young or old, could feel a sensation in their loins. Nobody had ever seen a man dance in the slow natural style with deliberate hip and body movements.

Whatever outpouring of empathy the mothers had towards Eric, morphed into total adoration towards Eric. The music played was designed to be slow. It was called, when a man loves a woman by Percy Sledge. Every eligible female asked Eric for a dance. Eric duly obliged all those who waited. With his prowess, he moved every sinew in his body to perfection. Soon afterwards, Eric's Sunday afternoons were taken up in his father's salmon coloured ford Zodiac that could be seen rocking sideways to sideways.

CHAPTER 2 : THE EMBASSY SPORTS DROME

The Embassy sports drome was immediately opposite the Harp club and therefore within a three-minute walk from 3 Palmerston road. The building had a rectangular shape on plan and a barrel-Vault shaped roof. With it being so close to the BSA (British Small Arms factory). It was a miracle that one of Adolf's many bombs failed to hit the place during the WW2. Although German bombs landed within the proximity of Gladstone, Palmerston and Grantham's roads thankfully, German bombers failed to hit the Embassy because the building became a major focal point after the WW2 for sporting events such as rollers skating, wrestling, music bingo to name a few. Every Saturday, after visiting the matinee at the Piccadilly picture house, we would visit the embassy roller skating rink where you could roller skated to your heart's content or until your body could take no more. It was sometimes difficult to get the roller skates to fit you which would eat into your roller skating time.

There was one song played over the speaker system again and again. People eventually complained about the choice being the same music Saturday after Saturday until one Saturday some irate customer broke the record. The song was called

'Windmill in Old Amsterdam'. The song was a sing-along about a mouse family living in an old Amsterdam windmill. The singer was a man named Ronnie Hilton and Parlophone records Ltd in 1964 released the song. I made new friends there, meaning boys and girls outside the circle of my school friends. Mom thought this was good because it broadened my horizons so I could build my confidence. Some of my friends had older friends who didn't seem to mix well and appeared to be on the periphery. One particular seedy-looking older man with teeth that had rarely seen the light of day decided to befriend me one Saturday and offered me free ice cream and to walk with me back to where I lived. He seemed a likeable character and a free ice cream is a free ice cream, and, so I agreed. When we arrived home, we both walked into the kitchen, where Mom was cooking again. Mom turned around and looked my new found friend from head to toe.

"And who might this be, May I ask?"

The silence was ominous, and before the utterance of another word, my mother delivered an unwashed saucepan between his eyes. His eyeballs went into reverse countless times. Eventually, he got to his feet again, and she gave him what she called a 'reminder'. She shouted at him as he ran out of the door.

"Don't be coming back, here again, ya dirty looking
Nancy boy or, I'll split ya into two, ya dirty ting"

The Embassy roller skate mornings were out of bounds for two months after that little episode.Every Monday night during the sixties, professional wrestling too place between 7:30pm to 10: 30.pm. Since we had no money to speak of, we schemed and plotted any possible way to gain access without paying the required entry fee of the five shillings. It took a few weeks but eventually both me and my older brother Seamus got in by virtue somebody leaving the fire escape door whenever the bouts started. We believe it was a serious non-smoker who loved wrestling but could not abide the smell of smoke or possibly knew the harmful effects smoking had on people.Having sneaked in, we made sure of keeping a low profile and stayed at the rear of the audience. The first night we managed to get in, I was quite scared and shocked at the number of people inside the sports drome and the amount of noise they were creating was horrendous. The lights would always be on full before the bouts started,then somebody would turn off the lights making everything dark and a spotlight beamed down from the ceiling into the corner of the drome. The loudspeakers on the wall started blasting out strange music, which aroused the crowd into a frenzy.

After a short while, the fever pitch escalated in to shouting abuse and other words we could not use inside school time. All of a sudden, two semi-naked men came out of the dressing room wearing what looked like their wife's, tightly fitted, brightly coloured knickers and a cape over their shoulders. While walking, towards a flood lit square positioned in the centre they passionately strutted their stuff. The ring had a canvass floor with ropes surrounding it. My brother told me the well-lit up area was called wrestling ring. With their tight knickers showing a well pronounced wife's wedding present, both wrestlers raised their hands in the air beckoning the crowd to shout more. One of the wrestlers was called'Billy Two Rivers.' This entitled him to wear feathers on his head, which symbolised that he was Red Indian, unlike the Asian Indians who bought your house next door. What shocked me was the number of women sitting in the first two row of seats. They sat there with the hair in rollers shouting far worse abuse than the men. They were not the wives of the wrestlers because I recognised some of them as neighbours living on Grantham and Gladstone road. Some of them were mothers to large families. How they could afford to get in was an absolute mystery to me! They would become every animated when they considered their pet wrestler was taking a beating or was at the end of some rough justice. At times it seemed to get out of hand. Women thought nothing of climbing into the ring and hand bagging a wrestler they disliked. Sometimes, they would wait for the moment a wrestler was lying on the edge of the canvass and run over and make every effort to pull the wrestlers wife's knickers off. The most poplar of all the local wrestlers were two brothers called John-Joe and Finbarr Raftery. John-Joe was the younger and smaller brother of Finbarr.

On many occasions during a tag-wrestling match he would be at the receiving end of a thrashing withFinbarr being unable to touch/tag. Had both men been able to touch then Finbarr was allowed to jump into the ring and take over his brother lame efforts. When John-Joe did manage to touch hands with Finbarr, his saviour, Finbarr would perform a triple for-ward summer-sault over the ropes or something similar and, somehow land on his feet and quickly release his little brother from being pun-ished. With John-Joe being able to run behind the ropes freeing Finbarr to 'make pure shite' of his two wrestling opponents. Upon seeing this act of brotherly salvation, the crowd entered into a false narcotic rapture. Wrestling theatrics was all part of the evening's entertainment. Some women thoroughly enjoyed watching men half murder each other, hoping that one day the same punishment might be handed out to their pathetic, drunken and pointless husbands of too many years!

The end of each wrestling match prompted a phalanx of men to walk either side of the wrestlers to protect them from the female malevolence. You would think the protection would be for over-eager amateur wrestlers with false courage fuelled by alcohol. Sometimes big-name wrestlers from London were invited to perform their physical theatrics. Wrestlers named Jackie Pallo, Adrian Street, Count Betelli, Mick McMannus the Royal brothers featured on the many posted billboards making it difficult to sneak in through the rear fire escape door. We managed, however, to get in and stand inconspicuously at the back. When the big names did appear, we noticed the crowd was more regional instead of local and minders who had cement bag shaped shoulders protected most of the guest wrestlers. TV cameras crews were always in attendance.

CHAPTER 2 :
THE FIGHT

One Saturday summer evening, my mother told me to take a walk with my friends to the park for a game of football. She said there was simply not enough room in the back garden.We all decided to walk to the park to play football when one of my friends noticed some tinker's damaging the front hedge to our home. It was put on me to give the cheeky bastard a hiding because we were both around the same age. The exchange of cuffs commenced at three o'clock that afternoon outside the house. I do not remember a heavyweight fight on TV lasting as long as ours. The longer the fight continued, the bigger the crowd. They formed a circle, clapped hands every time they thought their lad was winning and shouted across the fight ring whenever they wanted to put a bet on. I must have banged the Tinker's head against the front stone wall a hundred times and still he fought like an unemployed whore who had not received her client's money. We were biting, spitting, head butting kicking where possible, pulling of hair, bashing each other heads against the neighbours Austin A55 saloon car wheel hub-cap swearing-in brummy and quasi gaelic.Eventually I silenced him with an excellent secure head lock. I continued bashing his brains in with my other fist only to discover when I looked up, that I was surrounded by older tinkers looking and shouting down at my opponent to beat the shite out of me. I knew then that the odds were beginning to stack against me.

Worse still, my friends were nowhere in sight. The thought then went through my mind that I might not survive this fight, let alone, win it!! Suddenly the neighbour's wife came out of the house to go shopping. She looked around her husband's car and noticed some panel damage to the driver's side door and started to call the police. Once the Tinkers heard the word police, they all scarpered off like kippers on crack.

Before I could give the little bastard my final dig to the head, he managed to escape to fight another day. The fight must have gone on for ages because the people who didn't have sweets before the fight started had time to go down to the corner shop to buy sweets.My Dad's favourite sport was boxing. The only beneficial gift my Dad bought me was a pair of boxing gloves. However, in terms of boxing success I was a disappointment to him. He always imagined that I was going to be the next heavyweight champion of the world. Just like Sonny Liston. What made matters worse was the fact my uncle Joe on my mother's side, the man who had lied his way into the British army to escape poverty, had become a successful boxer whilst he was in the army. Dad had prophesied that I would undoubtably carry on the good work. I did attend amateur boxing clubs afterschool. Clubs like Wilmot Breeden and Small Health which permitted school boys to spar and train. The coaches had little time for school boys and spent most of their time coaching the older boxers to prepare for their forthcoming bouts. Therefore, my interest in boxing dwindled which was blessing in disguise.

CHAPTER 2 :
THE FLYOVER AT
CAMP HILL

One evening I read in the Birmingham Mail that the construction of a new flyover at the Camp Hill was near completion. The planners said it was there for a short period before the completion of a more permanent concrete structure. The man who built the temporary bridge was known to my mother because he was Irish and from the same county in Ireland. She told us in the kitchen one day that he used to run the Irish dances before WW2 at the Moseley Institute in Moseley before he ventured into construction. They both stayed in lodgings on the same road called Pearce Avenue in Olton near Solihull. He would always give her a lift home on his motorbike after the dances. He then started trading by the name of Jack O'Gallahan and ventured into construction with his brother Seamus and won a big project after the WW2 to take and remove all the tram rail lines in and around the Birmingham city centre. Mom said he was very greedy and ambitious. He always made a point of calling everybody by their first name. When people came to the site to talk to him, he would refuse to have anything to do with them if they did not arrive in a car.

Over the years he became enormously wealthy, and so did his immediate family. One day it was stated in the local press that a certain Mr O'Gallahan received a fine by the court for not declaring himself a millionaire. My Mom said knowing Jack that would mean he didn't want to declare himself a millionaire because he would need to pay more tax and, believe you me, Jack never was too fond of parting with his own money. She did say though Jack did pay for some Irish to be repatriated in the event of an early death.

I asked her if I could go with my friends on the bus into town so as we could be on the top deck of the bus when it drove over the flyover. She agreed, and five of us travelled into town on our own to come back again and ride over the flyover. When we came to the flyover approach ramp one of our friends decided to burst into tears screaming it was going to topple over. When we were at the top of the flyover, my two other friends starting vomiting when they looked out of the window. I thought to myself they don't get out very, much do they?

Two months after going over the Camp Hill flyover on a public bus with my friends, my mother told me I was going to have lessons in how to become an altar boy. That would mean I would need to go down to St Anne's church in Digbeth. St Anne's parish and the respective school had a headmaster at the time whose name was Mr Short. He had a smart daughter who went to St Paul's Grammar school for Girls then went on to a good university eventually ending up in politics and pinnacled her career as secretary of state for International Development of the U.k. She resigned over the Iraq war, saying that the premise for war was flawed and, the government were going to war without a clear mandate. What a pity others in the cabinet failed to quit and decided to continue to live off the gravy train. What a different place the world would be today.

I am sure my mother thought that the spiritual experience gained by me whilst training to be an altar boy would grant her absolution for all the sins, she may have committed vicariously or otherwise and could grant her an express ticket to the big man in the sky. Training to be an Altar boy entailed travelling to St Anne's on a Sunday evening for six weeks when everybody else was playing football. Learning when to ring the bell on the altar during the mass and other duties was the naturally excit-ing part of an altar boy's life. Trying to train me to learn Latin was not a good idea and, I went the first week begrudgingly, went the second week and faked illness on the third and never went there again. The woman who taught me whatever limited Latin I grasped came off the same shelf as Mrs Meehan without the heavy mascara makeup and surrounding recycled rouge.

CHAPTER 2 : THE WEEK THAT SHOULD NOT HAVE BEEN

At the beginning of the week I arrived home from school to listen to Mom inform us she had arranged ostensibly for a TV rental man to come over to discuss measures on how to reduce the rental cost of our black and white 12-inch T.V. What she was trying to do was the impossible. The impossible being to get us to stay in and start taking our homework duties more seriously. The man asked a large list of questions and numerous forms needed to be filled in. The gentleman told my mother that this was necessary because Palmerston Gladstone and Grantham Roads were notorious black spots. The TV company had rented out fifty TV sets and when they came to collect them at the end of the rental period nearly half of them had smashed or disappeared. Initially, we thought nothing of having a new device in the back of the TV called a slot machine. Over time the TV would switch itself off if the sixpence worth of entertainment ran its course. There was no way of telling accurately when the sixpence worth would expire, and TV would switch off just as the plot of the story was unfolding or when you were going to find out who was the killer in the end. The frustration of having entertainment on the drip was causing significant uneasiness, so we brokered a compromise between Mom and ourselves. We would do our homework on the understanding she didn't re-connect the sixpence slot machine.

The next day I narrowly avoided bumping into a policeman walking out of our house wearing a smile on his face. I immediately ran into the kitchen to ask Mom why had there been a policeman in our home. She told me my daft older brother Seamus had managed to obtain an air rifle from somewhere and thought it was funny to shoot at people from the first-floor bathroom window. He managed to shoot a labourer who was carrying a hod full of bricks on his shoulder up the ladder. The first shot my brother fired hit the hod carrier on the cheek of his backside. My naughty brother shot the hod carrier on the side blocked by bricks, so he did not have time to turn around to see where the shot originated. The second time he did know where the shot came from, as my brother was slower, hiding his head below the window cill. Rather than walking around to visit my mother, the labourers boss phone the police. I went into the bedroom to see my brother, and he had a face on him like a condemned man just waiting for the gallows.

In the middle of the same week I discovered Mr Paddon, my primary school teacher, told us he was leaving to teach elsewhere. He was a teacher who had the most significant influence on my life during my early years of junior schooling. He was the complete antipathy to Mrs Meehan - the bitch. He served as a soldier during and after WW2 and learned how to speak the German language. He taught the whole class how to sing Christmas carols in German and often talked to us in German or translated works from English to German and vice versa. One afternoon he spoke to us about a man called Jesus Christ of Nazareth or Jesus of Nazareth a Jewish and religious leader and preacher who according to him, came down from heaven to save the world from all it sins. He lived in the Middle East a place far away from England.

Mr Paddon told us Jesus was not a white man. Instead, he said he was the same colour as Ian. Ian was a small, dark-skinned boy who was on sick leave that day. He sat next to me in class. Up until that point, whether it was in the assembly when the headmaster preached the bible or in previous religious education lessons, we were never made aware of the colour of Jesus's skin. Until that point, I always thought his skin was the same colour as mine. I am sure to this day there are people in the UK and the USA who think Jesus was a white man. Perhaps if they understood the significance of the colour of a man's skin, there would be less ignorance and prejudice. Mr Paddon also told us Jesus didn't speak English or Arabic but spoke Aramaic. He also encouraged me to paint because I was always bringing in my art word work from home and painted whenever I could while in school. One rainy afternoon we were all kept in from the rain during lunchtime and I painted a horse so well that he gave me sixpence which was a lot of money for a primary school teacher.

At the end of every week Mom came in from shopping expedition. This meant she was carrying bags from Lady pool road to home. One weekend, she came in the house wearing a shocked ashen looking faced and was in a state of shock. We thought she had had her bag stolen, then we thought somebody had try to mug her then, finally, she muttered something incoherently and sat down on the settee. Dad thought of the only thing he ever thought about during his moments of crises and rushed over to the drink's cabinet open it and pulled out the Panacea of all Panacea - a bottle of Courvoisier cognac. I found his selection rather strange because Dad always pulled out the Remy Martin VSOP Cognac brandy. He quickly pulled a cork from the top of the bottle and poured what seemed to be a lot of brandy into Dad's special brandy glass. The kind of brandy glass reserved for his big drinking 'Towneys' whenever they visited the house for an afternoon of craic.

After a few minutes, Mom came around and found her second wind. She told Dad, while we were listening behind the door that she had been shopping up Lady pool road and while on her way home she noticed a seedy-looking large woman walking through the double doors of Woolworths carrying two large bags of groceries. A little man dressed as a manager followed her shouting, you're a thief, in her general direction; he then attempted to stop her from walking off. He must have been a brave man because he was only half her size and height. She turned around and dropped her bags on the floor. Before the bags could land on the ground, she had delivered the poor manager a head butt to the top of his head followed by a succession of blows to the body and head. The manager, with the help of gravity hit the ground heavily and lost consciousness. She then kicked him many times to his body and his head. She then picked up her shopping and left him there is a pool of blood. Other shoppers went over to see if he was still alive. The ambulance arrived and so did the police who started looking for witnesses. Mom was so shocked because she had not seen violence of that nature since the Second World War, and it brought back memories.

Approximately two months after the unpleasant shopping experience, I accompanied Mom to Ladypool road for the weekly shop. As we were walking up the left-hand side of the street looking in at shop windows, Mom noticed the same woman walking on the other side of the Lady pool and stared at her for a few seconds, then looked down at me and, held my hand securely.When I looked at the woman, I noticed a young boy by her side and seem to recognise him from the Saturday morning matinees. He was always in the middle of some sort of trouble causing issues with the staff and his peers. That boy eventually was expelled from secondary school ended up doing a full term in borstal and has been in and out of prison most of his life. In mitigation he didn't stand a chance in life. He fell from a tree as a youngster onto spiked railings causing him to have a metal plate inserted into his head and was lucky to be alive. His learning difficulties and mothers poor parentage in those days made life harder for him.

CHAPTER 2 :
THE ATTEMPTED
MUGGING

One balmy summer's evening, my father decided to walk back from the local pub after an evening of discussing work and pro-curing labour for his latest job site – Well, that's what he told my mother on more than one occasion. When he was about five meters from the front door of our house, three drunken burly Irishmen whose intentions were not good attempted to mug him. I could hear the men demanding money from Dad and, so, both myself and uncle Richard walked out of the house onto the pavement to see what was causing all the raucous. If you had never met my uncle Richard, you would soon realise that he re-sembled a passing ship in the night. He was the youngest of ten and said very little. You would swear he never wanted to speak because it might cost him sixpence per vowel. When it came to money, Richard was as tight as two coats of paint, timidly shy to a fault and, had a dreadful nose-picking habit after drinking a few bottles of Guinness.

The three gentlemen muggers wanted to relieve my father of all the money that lay deep within his pockets. Unfortunately, their foolishness knew no bounds, and the potential muggers were not aware of my father's ability to express himself both with his tongue and indeed very much so with his fists. Then something happened which I thought would never happen in a million years. Uncle Richard, the runt of the ten siblings shouted, in an uncharacteristically raised voice.

"If I take off my jacket! If I take off my jacket!"

He repeated this statement many times, so much so, I walked over to uncle Richard and stated that I would hold his jacket for him. I said it twice so that he understood what I was saying amid the mayhem. Without twisting or turning his body, he swivelled his neck slowly. He looked down at me, giving me an insane glazed look that only a man who had just filled his underwear with heifer's dust.

"Go away, ya fecking little eejit of a plebe and don't be hanging around here."

Upon hearing this direct instruction, I ran into the house to tell my mother about the commotion outside. She was inside in the kitchen cooking as usual, and, after listening to the messenger she dropped everything and quickly walked out through the front of the house only to find uncle Richard standing poised in the same position I left him in. His jacket still on his shoulders, his hands in his pockets, and Dad just finishing expressing himself with his fists.

The three motionless bodies had the appearance of dying ants at the end of summer. My mother was not best pleased and looked at my Dad.

"What is going on here Jim?"

"Oh, Mary, he said in a lilt I had never heard before. These poor creatures are paralytic." he said with wry smile.

"Look at the poor creatures. Aren't they just after losing their way in life and have drank too much for their good!"

Mom stared at my Dad for what appeared to be an excessive amount of time and said.

"That's it Jim !!!" she announced with authority.

"We are not living here another week longer in this neighbourhood. Everybody is moving out, and it is no place to raised children. We will start looking for houses up the hill towards Hall Green the day after tomorrow."

And so, it was, the search for a safer neighbourhood started in earnest. It was interesting to observe the clashes of wills. Dad said he wasn't too concerned when it came to locating the perfect dwelling. Nonetheless, Mom discovered that the Dads 'laissez-faire' approach to searching altered if the proposed new house was not within proximity of a public house that serves a good pint of Guinness. Ultimately, Mom wanted a home in a safe leafy suburb within walking distance of the supermarket because she had experience hardship in Ireland and viewed graphically the trauma caused by the horrors of working through the Second World War.

CHAPTER 2 : THE BIG MOVE

After many months of searching for a suitable new residence, the McEvilly scouts spotted a four-bedroom semi-detached house which would be appropriate for all those willing to move up the hill. Moving the McEvilly possessions lock stock and barrel from Sparkbrook to Hall Green was not a simple affair. It was similar to the popular TV series running at that time called 'The Beverly Hills Billies' countless trips were made from Sparkhill to Hall Green to transfer timber from the garage to the garden in Hall Green.

The very English neighbours watched in astonishment when we all (meaning Mom, Dad, six children, one uncle, and not forgetting one unloved mongrel mute) arrived in the leafy suburb. Prince the mute perpetrated the first infringement by refusing to accept a collar and lead like every other dog in posh Hall Green. Prince, being Prince, was streetwise and, therefore, would wait for the front door to open and then run out to canine freedom. This freedom meant he was gone all day and would only return home in the early hours of the following morning when everybody was asleep in their beds. His early morning barking was an irritant to the neon middle classes of Hall green's leafy street suburban residents giving to several complaints. He also managed singlehandedly to increase the illegitimate canine population of Hall Green and adjourning districts. As the saying goes.

"Big dogs' small tails, little dogs all tails."

It was only a matter of time before our neighbours in Hall Green colloquially referred to Prince as the 'Dog with two willies'.

Unlike Sparkbrook, you could not run down to the local store and pick up some items. Everything needed to be arranged and organised. Shopping needed completing in one go, with everything bought for the week. Many of the shops were family-owned. One shop, in particular, had a very proud Englishman as its owner. Mom said he always bragged about how smart his children were and how well they were progressing at the local grammar school and mentioned many times that he had a boat hiring business on the south coast. One day she went into the shop to buy some meat and asked if could have a closer look at the role of beef in the shop window.

"I don't think it's big enough" to which the shop proprietor responded.

"It is good enough for your lot isn't it?"

My mother never used the shop again. I suppose the only way to manage folk like him is to hit him in the pocket. She also could not understand why so many of the neighbours would ply their faces with makeup and get all dressed up to go out shopping. Wives wearing fresh makeup and white gloves would push clean and polished prams to the parade of shops. Then they would return with a small amount of shopping. She called it the 'Kippers and curtains brigade'.

The new suburban neighbours had the same money we had. However; they were better at surviving on a thrifty budget. Perhaps their budget did not include alcohol or cigarettes. They showed impeccable manners, a willingness to listen to you when you talked to them. With the virtues of quietness, politeness and dignity, a sense of class prevailed.

We had arrived in middle-class England.

CHAPTER 3 : THE GRAND STORE

J ack and Bridie O'Rourke's general store is located on the main road leading out of Birmingham, generally heading south towards Stratford Upon Avon. The store purchased in the early 1960s had everything a man in the street primarily needed, including fresh Irish food, a much sought-after product by the Irish community in and around the area.

My mother happened to be close friend, and Towney of Mr's. O'Rourke thought it might be a good idea for me to work in their shop on a part-time basis as her husband was asking around to see if anybody was available to help. The O'Rourke's were shrewd when it came to matters relating to money. It was rumoured that they owned at least twenty properties scattered in and around the Sparkbrook and Sparkhill areas, all of which amassed via scrimping and saving. They wouldn't, therefore, not want anybody handling their money they did not trust or indeed know well. My mother, in her wisdom, volunteered my services, and I was duly despatched to the store one night, not knowing very little about the finer points of successful retailing. I worked two evenings after school the first week for which Mr's. O'Rourke thrust two half-crowns into the palm of my hand at the end of the second evening. With me being a naive eejit, I became very excited over this windfall which made run all the way home and give my mother the two half-crowns not realizing I had left myself short on the deal. I suppose working in a shop instead of doing homework was not so bad because I shared work duties with a classmate from school who happened to be the O'Rourke's nephew.

During our first shift together, he showed me that family loyalty had its limits when we both consumed an infinite number of chocolate bars and soft toffees. We gained great satisfaction from this greed. And of course, so did the lining the pockets of the local dentist who would greet us with a smile. At times Jack reacted with excitement when he saw more than three customers waiting in the shop. He would take it upon himself to rush in after serving the vegetables outside and without washing his hands rush behind the counter. Occasionally, while rushing in to serve behind the counter he would leave his cigarette butt balancing it on the edge of the counter. He took great pleasure in slicing the rashers of Irish bacon, allowing the bacon to drop into the palm of his hand and then fall on to the greaseproof sheet paper. Finally, he'd throw the greaseproof paper on the weighing scales. Most times the bacon weigh was more than the customer needed, he could easily convince them the bacon was the finest from Ireland and in big demand. He never knew the accurate price of the bacon. It was only when a customer did not repeat his custom did Jack realise, he had overcharged.

CHAPTER 3 : THE GENTLEMAN

Now and again, perhaps twice a week, a huge black man with a friendly demeanour would come into the shop to purchase a large number of 2lb bags of sugar. Sometimes the number of sugar bags would double. Somebody mentioned he was brewing alcohol; nobody was bothered, most noticeably, the O'Rourke's as they were gaining well from his particular transaction. This arrangement went on for several months. Then, one evening the same gentleman came into the shop to purchase more sugar bags and while on his way out he crossed paths with a group of scantily clad females talking to each other with heavy Dublin accents. It would seem from where I was serving vegetables outside these women were from the unsociable side of Dublin.

The outcome of these two parties crossing paths was not one of serendipity but one of listening to an uncontrolled verbal and racial abuse towards this gentleman with their vile and ugly tongues. This abuse went on for several minutes. The gentleman stood there motionless with a face showing great hurt and embarrassment. He then walked with dignity back to his address. I thought to myself it's far more difficult to hurt a man in a fight than to beat him through the aid of a wicked mind and a nasty tongue. If ever you want to destroy a big man and bring him to his knees, don't kick him where it hurts or punch him in the face - racially abuse him. When I returned home from work early evening, I told my mother what happened. She told me it was not uncommon to see and witness horrible things being said, especially between those people who should know better. I wondered where does such evil and hatred emanate? How can people not understand how important a persons heritage is to them? The great paradoxid is from what I witnessed in my short life was the majority of racism or bigotry exist amongst immigrants through no fault of their own. After the little episode between the ladies, who were not so ladylike and, the aggrieved gentleman, I always added one or two extra bags of sugar to his order.

Most evenings during, the week large Irishmen the size of a house entered the shop and ordered Irish food. The shopping list consisted of Irish sausages, rashers of the best of gammon, with Irish cheese and irish butter and of course soda bread which was their staple diet. This shopping list represented the staple diet of these hard-working manual labourers who come over from their native Ireland. The majority of these men lived a bachelor existence living alone in houses with multi-let rooms with nobody other than themselves to prepare their dinner after a long day's manual sweat. Whatever opportunities they had to meet a suitable colleen on a Saturday night at the Shamrock dance would be made difficult through virtue of a low level horizontal brass positioned only six inches from the dance floor. For a man to have any chance of gaining a dance, he would need to step over the bar and take one step forward, stretch his hand and ask the waiting colleen to accompany him in the dance floor. The problem with this approach was that the woman was provided the opportunity to appraise the state gentleman who was proposing to be her next dance partner.

One stumble or sign of drink or dirty hands or fingernails would constitute an instant rejection. Many of these men would need to have a drink to muster up enough courage to ask a woman for a dance in the first place. Many of these women harboured snobbery only the Irish could experience. The pretension of ownership meant a man could be more successful in gaining a woman's hand for a dance. After which an opportunity arose, allowing questioning by the women inquiring into the gentleman's suitability and background. 'Land or a farm back in Ireland?' Many Irish women dreamed their man would be tall, dark, handsome with land in Ireland. A farm in Ireland meant a passport back away from the miserably crowded city and unnatural living conditions. Birmingham had little to offer in return to their native lush green pastures where food tasted fresher, life was more relaxed, more user-friendly, and, where the pressure of work would not be allowed to impact on the Irish lifestyles' tranquillity.

CHAPTER 3 : MR GAFFNEY

Every Friday and Saturday evening around 8 o'clock, a huge man, the size of a giant, would walk down Long Street, passed O'Rourke's general, and walk on towards Sparkhill. He must have been twenty-five stone, the shoulders of Ox, and fists the size of Watermelons. Customers informed me his name was Martin Gaffney.

He was from Galway, where all the hardest and finest of men originated. He lived up Long Street with his wife and eight children and owned many of ponies, which were free to graze in some large fields out in Earlswood. His evening job was being a bouncer at the Irish dance hall in Walford Road Sparkbrook, opposite the roller skate ring. His size and fearsome looks terrified me so much, so I would run into the shop and out the back to avoid him. I dreaded the day he might walk into the shop to buy food and, we didn't have it on the shelf. Three men either side with two to three men walking behind him always accompanied him. I suppose he had quite a cult following including other back slappers waiting for his arrival at the dance venue where they would buy him drinks most of the night. Many a drunken man walked into the dance hall looking for trouble, and many men needed to be removed by stretcher after Mr. Gaffney had dealt his brand of discipline on them. Many men from Dublin known as Jackeens would enter the dance looking for trouble. Nonetheless, the men from the West with the help on Mr. Gaffney would send them on the way in a horizontal position. One night, three sailors were paying the entrance fee into the dance and just mentioned to Mr. Gaffney he should get some 'Ugly fat off himself'. All three ended up outside, looking up at the stars.

Organized bare-knuckle fistfights took place in fairgrounds and warehouses. The funding and organizing of such events were a matter for the underworld. Mr. Gaffney was undefeated. One fight, in particular, made the Evening Mail because it had attracted so many spectators. The match was between Mr. Gaffney and a certain Mr. McGarry. Mr. McGarry had arrived in good stead because he had just won the Golden Gloves amateur boxing competition held in the USA. However, the fight did not take place because the police got to know about it through their informants and, they put a stop to it.

When I told the story to my Dad about a colossus of a man called Mr. Gaffney walking passed the shop twice a week. He told me he knew him when he arrived from Ireland, and when he first married. Dad said he was a nice good-hearted family man who attended St Anne's church in Digbeth with all his children. He was an outstanding amateur boxing champion at thirteen stones. However, the years of standing at a door undertaking the dance owners' dirty work had taken its toll. Martin was known for being very Irish, which meant he would empty his pockets and buy you a drink, but if you upset him, he would throw you out the dance hall headfirst. Then again, if you had no money to buy breakfast the following morning, he would still give you money without expecting in return. As the years went by, nature had its way. Very little was known then about the hidden dangers of obesity, and Mr. Gaffney suffered through ignorance when his toes turned black and needed to be amputated. Later his ankle was amputated, and then his foot and the rest are history. He died at fifty-two years of age. Dying young is the price you pay for being too busy looking after everybody's wealth.

On a winter's Sunday morning, Mr. O'Rourke arranged to meet me at the rear garden of some derelict property on the other side of the Stratford Road, immediately opposite his shop. After waiting for ten minutes, he rolled up in his dirty brown van and what appeared to be his Sunday suit. He jumped out of his van and opened the back doors and put on some overalls.

"Morning Gasureen, here now, here are some brown paper bags for you. Go over there to that pile of coke and start filling up the bags."

I stared at Mr. O'Rourke and then looked at the pile of coke lying there.

"It states smokeless coke on the side of the bags. The coke over there is not smokeless, Mr. O'Rourke."

I then remember my mother mentioning something about the government bringing in new laws regarding the burning of non-smokeless coke. Mr. O Rourke looked at me with a annoyed face.

"Don't be looking at me in that tone of voice!"

I thought for a moment about what he had just said and responded by saying.

"Don't you mean don't be talking to me in that tone of voice?"

To which he finished buttoning his overalls.

"Now, Young fella! Don't be smart and stop giving out old guff to me, or I tell ya father that yourself and the other young buck were puffing away on those woodbine cigarettes around the back of the shop."

I paused for thought.

"Enough said?"

I started filling the non-smokeless coke into the new bags bearing the smokeless logo. I had about six bags filled when I heard the lower casement of a window pulling up, and a vexed-looking woman with curlers in her hair poked her head out. She started ranting on to Mr. O'Rourke about not wanting to listen to the sound of voices and shovels scraping the ground early on the sabbath.

Mr. O'Rourke was having none of it.

"Stick your ugly face back inside where it belonged, well out of the way in case somebody might think the local slaughterhouse had relocated."

This of course did not help the simmering confrontation between the two sparring partners. The woman then said she was going to phone the Police. Mr. O'Rourke told me to take plenty of no notice and hurry up and fill the bags. Mr. O'Rourke knew the residents of Sparkbrook were too lazy to check to see if the coke was smokeless providing it was within the family budget.

I filled around twenty bags and loaded them into the van. Mr. O'Rourke then told me to go to the shop and help out with serving behind the counter. It was 12:30 when a rather sizeable uniformed police officer darkened the doorway of the shop. He waited for me to finish serving a customer.

"Whereabouts of a certain Mr. O'Rourke?"

I told him I didn't know, but he was not far away because his dirty brown van was parked outside. After about ten minutes, Jack came walking in through the shop front door. I pointed to the policemen and said.

"He needs to talk to you about something."

I had a good idea what it was about and Bridie, his wife, who was standing next to me behind the counter, asked me.

"What is that man doing in the shop at this time of a Sunday morning?"

"I have not a clue Bridie."

"Well, it must be vital for him to be here this time on a Sunday morning."

Mr. O'Rourke asked the policemen to follow him into the back of the shop. Meaning there was a discussion to be had behind closed doors. The two of them were in there for eternity. You could hear the odd bouts of laughter with chuckles being shared then, suddenly, the door opened. The policemen walked unsteadily and in a gingerly manner. He seemed to stop and straighten himself up before he was presentable. He walked through the shop, brushing against the tray containing the Irish soda bread and then veered to the other side of the shop and collided with the counter and, finally made a successful beeline to the front door. He managed successfully to open the door in his state of drunkenness. Bridie was not too happy with what she had witnessed and gave her husband a fierce tongue lashing as only an Irishwoman would issue before a novena.

Jack said, "Sure what harm Bridie?" and went on to say he knew his father well.

"He was a policeman in Castlebar in Mayo and loved a drop of the holy water now and again!"

When Jack went his ways, she asked me to go into the back and clean up the mess. I found a half bottle of Tullamore whisky with the top off. I went into the back to search for the holy water to no avail. Oh well, it is just as well, the holy water would have finished him off. The early afternoon before the shop closed, Jack attempted to measure the glass area to the shop front door. The very glass that was damaged by the non-compo's mentis policeman slamming the door on his way out. I counted the number of times Jack returned to measure the glass area without actually writing the dimensions on a piece of paper. It was seven times, to be exact. It reminded me of a long-running BBC Comedy TV series featuring comedians, Arthur Haines, Nicholas Parsons, and Dermott Kelly. Perhaps, Jack did have a drop of the holy water after the young policemen departed.

CHAPTER 3 : THE MOLLOYS

There is tiny remote village near a one-horse town called Glenna Maddi somewhere in the county of Galway. Here Mr and Mrs Molloy elected to stretch the physical elasticity of a woman's body by producing the finest of children, eighteen in total. Life was such that for them to entertain themselves, they would spend most afternoons not going to school. Instead, they threw stones at each other from afar. (Pegging) This form of physical entertainment was an alternative means of entertainment popular, because it didn't cost money. This way of life continued until the children matured into an income-earning adolescent. Then it was off, to England they would travel to follow their brothers and sisters before them with five pounds in their pockets. The eldest of them was called big Tony, and he decided to make his fortune in the bright lights of Birmingham,. Known as a city of a thousand trades and recognised for easy employment, meaning you could leave you a job in the morning and find another job in the afternoon. Birmingham manufactured everything from an engine to a pin. Big Tony secured himself a position driving a wagon shifting excavated muck from the big holes in the city to the council tip and sometimes to the fly-tip depending on what mood he found himself.

On a Sunday big Tony, along with his other brothers, would make their way the Irish Club in Town called the White Elephant. The club was an all-day drinking club in the centre of town. Inside were two big roulette tables, lots of smaller tables for a man to play the Irish card game of 'Twenty-five'. Other tables where a man, if he so fancied, could play poker and above all the place was open all day Sunday just like Ireland.

Back in Emerald isle a man could get a 'lock in' your man's pub, which meant he could drink most of the day providing he closed the curtains and didn't talk politics. Regrettably and, most unfortunately, no roulette tables, poker tables, nor, indeed, ladies of the night. His release from the shackles of the Catholicism and the relentless cruelty of rural poverty gave him newfound freedom and a need to prove his true worth in the new bold world outside of Ireland. This determination to prove oneself came in the form of seeking a fortune, which was more and more difficult to come by as the years passed with visits to the White elephant becoming more and more frequent. All-day Sunday drinking followed by having Monday off to have the 'Hair of the hound' known to those who indulged in such hedonism as the Monday club. This special club saw a vast amount of slurping and, equally, vast amounts of monies gambled away. It was only when a man came to his senses did, he realise he was the subject of his own vices. Sometimes the road to Damascus happens too late for some, and for others, it was a much-welcomed saviour.

I first encountered big Tony Molloy on a wet Monday lunchtime when he poured himself into O'Rourke's shop looking a peculiar colour. He immediately followed by seven of his siblings. They walked in and asked with great urgency.

"Where were the crated bottles of Lucozade?"

Upon receiving a response to the question, a rapid movement of bodies took place. Once the slurping of the first bottle of Lucozade finished a new complexion on the day featured, and the gravitas of the situation subsided. It was only when each man had slurped themselves midway down a third of a bottle of Lucozade would some kind of decipherable conversation commence. The craic would start about the great day they had in the White Elephant the day before and how they all missed home and the fresh food and the famous Irish breakfast, which was slurped down the help of fresh milk. Mr O' Rourke sometimes came into the shop and, the topic of conversation would change from the craic the previous day to the price of heifers, pigs, and hay could be had in and around the best market towns in Galway and surrounding counties. They would talk about Gaelic football teams and Hurley and why the Dublin folk (Jackeens) always thought they had the best team. Then it was the turn of Irish politics and the differences between voting for Fine Gael, or Fianna Fail. With their tongues twittering and their bodies hung-over the conversation continued deep into the subject at hand. I never understood Irish politics, nor indeed English politics. I could never tell if they actually knew anything about politics or indeed if they knew anything about Irish Politics. Conversations ended with the unceremoniously gulping down of the last bottle of milk. According to one of the men swallowing it, milk was the finest medicine any doctor could ever prescribe you. Milk put a lining on their stomachs, preventing a hung-over feeling when they eventually ventured back to work on Tuesday. Before finally departing one of the Molloys went on to mention Martin Muldoon was seen for a few hours seated in his rightful place in the White Elephant. The deferent listening lads smiled at each other with silence and pride. Suddenly a younger and more innocent member of clan asked, who was Martin Muldoon? The older men looked at each other in astonishment!

Martin Muldoon had a large cult following because of his infamy and outrageous behaviour. Martin had not worked since he departed from his native Galway twenty years prior. If Martin was in the club drinking all day it was because he had latched onto somebody who would buy him double brandies all day so as to listen to his tales of the past. It would seem, he had never paid for drinks when in the White Elephant because he had a notorious reputation, for being a rogue and, the Irish always love a rogue or anti-establishment figure. He was known for either causing or being in the middle of all fights in the Irish dance halls. He was a man who found it all too easy to mug poor, hard-working Irish lads returning home on a Friday night with a week's pay packet in the front trouser pocket. Muldoon's reputation followed him from place to place wherever the Irish decided to populate throughout the UK. There were rumours he took part or was indeed instrumental in several bank robberies and served a number of sentences for doing so. One story rolls out that Martin, being a typical rogue, would network with other rogues who were not necessarily on his manor. One Friday night, he went down to the smoke to purchase and transport several sticks of dynamite meant for blowing a bank safe. He met up with a gang from the East End to purchase several sticks of dynamite. However, it was not the only thing he bought. Martin was fond of a drop of brandy and managed to pour half a bottle down his throat during the course of the evening while enjoying the company of the criminal fraternity. This was, of course, not the most intelligent thing to do and, so, there he was, with his belly full of brandy, heading towards Birmingham via the new M1 motorway.

Unfortunately for Martin, London in the 1950s suffered from unwelcomed visits of thick fog known as 'peasoupers'to the people of London. With his accompanying full belly, Martin drove his van carrying sticks of explosives around and around in the thick smoke for hours. Until, eventually, he gave up the idea of returning home that night and parked his van up to have asleep. The following morning Martin was awakened by a tap on the car door window. Who was it but a rather inquisitive police officer. Martin, in all his wisdom, had unknowingly parked his car a hundred and fifty yards away from the Prime Ministers official residence - Number Ten Downing Street. Martin was sent down for five years because he could not convince the judge the sticks of dynamite were for demolitions of old building works up in Birmingham. The judge suggested it was for more sinister purposes.

Martin's retentions at her Majesty's pleasure were many. Mainly because he was let down by others involved but, on this occasion, Martin was at fault. When picked up at the prison gate after serving his time, the taxi driver asked him.

"Would he go to prison again?" To which he responded.

"Most certainly not!!"

I suppose prison gives a man plenty of time to think and can eventually change a man, I pondered behind the counter. Muldoon had managed prostitutes, bit off men's ears and fingers, was a hired thug even bit off a man's nose because he would not share his sausage with him at breakfast and many more criminal activities.

Before leaving the shop Mr. O'Rourke would thank them a million and see them out the door where they had a short walk over the Angel or Vic public house. He was glad to see them out the door but, at the same time, he did enjoy the banter.

CHAPTER 3 : TALK OF THE TOWN

The Talk of the Town was an all-day drinking club situated on the Stratford road Sparkbrook mid-way between fifteen terraced shops and places of business. The building itself had seen better days and was no oil painting. Indeed, the upper floor bay windows looked tired and should have had a lick of paint fifteen years earlier. Two Irishmen owned the place. One of the owners was a wrestler. He was well known for his televised wrestling appearances every Monday night at the Embassy Roller Rink located around the corner in Walford road. The second owner was an uncanny type nicknamed 'The Hat' because he was not proud of his baldness; rumours had it he went to bed with his hat on. The front of the building was like most speakeasy clubs you see in the films. It had the same fascia as those you would see in the Chicago gangster films. No windows at ground level, only a narrow front door with a small opening which operated by sliding a piece of wood across an aperture whenever it suited the doorman. To gain access to the drinking club, you needed to know the password. The doorman would always ask you.

"Are you a member, sir?" You would respond by saying. "Yes! I am!"

The password never changed in forty years of trading. As such, anybody who did not know the password was not a regular customer or a local. One Saturday afternoon, Mr. O'Rourke asked me to assist him with delivering groceries with his van, which meant carrying boxes full of groceries to the actual place of delivery. We initially dropped groceries off in and around Farm Park Road, and then we went to Grantham road to deliver more groceries, and finally, we went to the Talk of the Town.

Mr. O'Rourke stopped and parked his van on the main Stratford road, which of course, was not allowed and asked me to take a tray full of food into the Club. He walked with me to the door and rang the bell for me. We both waited with me holding the tray of food in my hands. The little sliding timber slot pushed to one side, and a voice said, 'Are you a member sir?' I looked around to see if Mr. O'Rourke would say yes only to find he had returned to his van and was preparing to start the engine and drive off. 'Yes, I am a member' and continued to shout through the aperture; there was a delivery of food for the Club. The door opened in response and a burly unshaven bald, ugly man with piercing blue eyes, and a desperate Dan chin blocked the doorway. With a heavy bread tray getting heavier by the second, he asked, without looking at me.

"What da ya want? Ya, little bollocks!"

I told him "I had a tray of food from O'Rourke's general grocery store!"

"Delivery?" He said, "What does yeah mean? I didn't order any delivery?"

"Perhaps somebody else did?"

"Huh, what have ya in that fecking bread tray of yours anyhow?"

"Well, mister, there is." I nervously replied.

"Sliced white bread ham, cheese, gammon, sliced onions and four packets of Kerry Gold butter!"

"Who ordered this stuff?" He then looked down into the dark hallway and shouted,

"Mick, come here will ya, ya old eejit? Who ordered this food?"

Mick answered. "How would I know, sure, I only just after returning from God's country after burying me poor old mother."

"In any case, we need food here for sure; the lads are starving, and their spending well on the roulette table and the women?"

Another door opened, and I could see people sitting at a round table staring at a roulette table-turning endlessly. It reminded of the casinos you would see on TV or at the Piccadilly or Walldorf cinemas. A large, powerfully built bald man sporting a week-old stubble came out of the room and closed the door behind him. He then stood standing with his back leaning against the wall and reeked of I love my perfume. He then pivoted his massive torso on to a tall bar stool and reached his arm out to touch the other wall and slowly turned his head towards me and started scratching his chin slowly. He then took the tray off me and walked into a separate room.

I was beginning to realise by just looking and listening at my tender age of thirteen, that this place was no confessional box. I was in fact in a house of Gaelic iniquity where an Irishman's brain is overlapped by his foreskin whenever, he could afford it. A place where a man's intention would be not to go home to his lonely lodging which he shared with others but to make every effort to bury Fagan into one of the available women, affectionately referred to as Sligo Kate and Tipperary Mary to name but a few. These lost souls or ladies of the night were slurping their drinks, laughing out loud against the clinking of half-full glasses of Champagne with whoever had the time and money to spend on them. I had heard an awful lot of gossip outside the Club about what was happening inside the Club, and it all seemed to be rolling out more or less like the rumors were true. I witnessed another lady lying flat out on the staircase in an uncompromising posture with lots of what seemed to be small empty beer bottles labelled Guinness and Harp.

Several minutes passed when suddenly through the door leading from the bar itself came the man with the shaven head. He looked at me as if he was about to consume me with his eyes.

"What da ya fucking meen coming in here with an I owe note?"

I tried to explain to him I was only the delivery boy and I didn't know about O'Rourke's IOU note. He was most dismissive and wouldn't hear any of it. He then picked me up with one hand with his clench fist and used the wall to raise me above his head slowly.

"Now listen here, Gasureen, you and that bastard O'Rourke have as much chance of getting money out of meeee as I have of sand-papering a lion's arsehole!!, Now feck off will ya!"

Sparkbrook teaches you to be wise at an early age and not to give smart answers. However, on this occasion, I did and, as I ran out the door near to tears, I shouted back.

"You are a big thick fat pig of an ugly bully you can't even speak the Irish language!!"

I went straight home after the Talk of the Town episode. I didn't tell my mother as some issues are better not talked about, and, I certainly didn't tell my father!! I have always believed that if you live by the sword then, you shall die by the sword. Several years later that big fat brute had a dispute with a beer delivery driver over a simple issue of a truck scratching his car. It transpired there was an exchange of words and, the delivery driver who happened to be a large gentleman with pride to match his courage climbed out of his cab to settle matters with a quick exchanged of cuffs. Unfortunately for him, he was unaware that the bald man was a trained wrestler. A few minutes later, the delivery driver was laid out on the floor. He spent the next three weeks in the hospital, most of which were in intensive care. There was an investigation by the police and the employer, but there were no witnesses. So, the bald thug got away with it or, so he thought! The unions got to know about one of their fully paid up member's plight and decided to boycott all deliveries to the Club. As a consequence, he had no option other than to sell his Club twelve months later at a significant loss.

CHAPTER 3 : WORKING AT MORRISONS THE BUTCHERS

During the time I worked at the O'Rourke's general grocery store, I decided to have a break and work for somebody else on a part-time basis and to see if the grass was greener on the other side. I started looking around other shops in the local area and noticed an advert on the shop window of a butcher called Morrisons. The shop was part of a long line of shops linked together running either side of Lady pool road. I went inside to find out more details, and the owner talked to me and asked me questions about my experience. I told him that I had work experience during my stay at O'Rourke's shop. He agreed to take me on a full day Saturday starting at eight in the morning and to work until six in the evening. What he didn't tell me was that I would be washing display trays for most of the day in the back which meant I would be leaning over a Belfast sink without seeing the light of daylight.

As if that was not bad enough, they found out that I had an Irish name and working conditions took a turn for the worst. There were about eight employees, of which most of them served at the shop counter with two making deliveries. Every time they walked into the back to give me a tray to wash they had great delight in muttering some obscenity about the Irish. Referring to me as a 'Duck egg' or a 'Catholic bastard' or others some other unpleasant names it dawned on me that this was the first time, I had come upon the true English or should I say the true Brummie narrow mindedness. Until that point in my life, I went to school with Irish or Irish descent children and worked for the O'Rourke's in their shop. I never thought of people as being anything else but my equal. Strangely, I was taught the majority of the time by English Catholics they, who I found to be the nicest of folk to all people. I worked there for two Saturdays, and I told Mr Morrison that two days was enough for me. He asked me why I was leaving and I told him for a better job. I would have told him anything to get away from the place.

I don't think Mr Morrison was a racist because he was working out what he owed me for my two Saturdays and he asked me how many brothers and sisters did I have? I consider the question to be a fair and reasonable and in my book a man like that is indeed not a racist. I went home that night and never told my parents why I only worked two days at Morrisons and so I was more than happy to return to O'Rourke's to serve customer Irish food.

CHAPTER 3 :
IRISH MATH'S

One balmy midsummer evening a man came into the shop looking tired . I recognized him as one of the stores weekly customers who would always purchase Irish food in a quietly spoken voice and then go about his business. He was of stocky build and well over six feet tall. I seem to remember his first name as being Finbarr. He asked me in a very calm manner.

"Was Jack around anywhere?"

I said to him 'He is in the back looking at some invoices. I will go and get him. He said that's fine I will wait here.

I went into the back and told him about the big man in the shop asking for O'Rourke. Jack balanced on one foot and stretched his neck by three inches to see around the boxes that were concealing him from the public.

"That's OK! It's your man Finbarr O'Toole! He a fine Lad, sure he is from Mullingar, itself."

"How are yeah, Finbarr?" enquired O' Rourke as he walked out the back into the shop.

"Well, Mr. O'Rourke, I will be fine once you have answered my question." said O' Toole with a tone of voice slightly more authoritarian.

"Well, Yesterday I bought twelve eggs, one large soda round loaf, two packs of Kerry gold butter, two pints of milk, two pounds of gammon rashers tin of Irish tea, cabbage and potatoes, and err, twelve Ribs and, you charged me one pound eighteen shillings and five pennies."

"Now jack, that seems an awful amount of money for so little and, it is more than what yeah charged me the week before, yeah?"

"Right!!" said, Jack "I'll get behind the counter and check those prices for yeah!"

Jack hurriedly walked behind the counter and ducked his head below the counter level and, after about thirty seconds, suddenly jumped into the air providing a two-inch space between the shop floor and the soles of his feet.

"Well, Finbarr! I have checked the price list, and the prices are correct!"

"OK" said, O'Toole "If you say that's correct, then that's fine by me, Mr. O'Rourke!"

O'Toole did a swivel and within seconds, walked out of the shop to quench his thirst with a pint of Guinness.

Once O'Rourke returned to the rear of the shop, I walked quickly behind the counter to serve whoever might come into the shop. Meanwhile, alas, my curiosity got the better of me, and I started looking for the price list O'Rourke looked up when he was bending down. I looked, and I looked because I might need it when queried on a price. I even picked up Mrs. O'Rourke's famous green credit book, which had the appearance of a ledger book. I looked in the book for the first time to see if the prices could be found, to no avail. Then I started looking through every page and noticed there was no index, no alphabetical order, plenty and misspelt names and ninety percent of the writing was illegible.

The writing was at varying angles, colors and sizes but all with the hand of one writer as cryptical as a crossword puzzle. I once heard an English neighbor tell my Dad. Sigmund Freud asserted the Irish mind was unfathomable. I must confess after reading the O'Rourke Credit book; he may have a point.

I felt sorry for O'Toole because he was typical of the poor. As the adage states, it is only the rich who argue over money. The poor are too proud to do so.

CHAPTER 4 :
JOURNEY TO IRELAND

Between the ages of five to fifteen, when other children went on holiday with their parents to Pontins or even to visit relatives' over-seas, we were religiously shipped back to our grandparent's farms in Ireland, which meant trapping us in a love-hate relationship. We loved the preparation, planning and experiencing the journey but, sometimes found the isolation and solitude of farm life challenging. However, assisting in the processing of the harvest and bringing in the turf for the winter months reduced the bordom.

Farm life had little in common with the way we lived our lives for the remainder of the year and, its location was at times an unsociable distance to the nearest town of Castlebar. The Journey to Ireland took place each year during July. Sometimes four members of the McEvilly's family would travel, and sometimes it would be five members. The total number would average ten when you included Mrs. O'Rourke and some of her children. Sometimes Mr. O'Rourke would take us to the station in his big brown grocery van or Dad would if he wasn't busy. Invariably we were rushing around at the last minute, packing our bags loading them into the van and organizing sandwiches. Once loaded, the van and its occupants travelled at speed up the Stratford road towards the city down into Digbeth and onto the cobbled station entry road that bisected New Street Station. With all our bags offloaded and placed on the tarmac adjacent to the railway track, we would wait in anticipation for a massive noisy black mechanical device called a steam engine to slowly enter the station. With it came volumes of belching white smoke coming from its' chimney and loud steam noises from its undercarriage. Once we had climbed the steep steps into the carriage, we were told to claim a seat while the adults arranged the loading of heavy suitcases into the storage areas and overhead racks.

Before the train departed from the station, it was customary for Mrs. O'Rourke to conduct a ceremony which ensure a safe journey to Ireland. This involved the communal five our Fathers, ten Hail Marys and a sprinkling of Holy water. An additional splash was sometimes necessary for those she suspected of not washing their faces or avoided washing behind their ears. The train then pulled slightly to the front, and you could hear the sound of carriage buffers clattering, and then slowly moving through the long unlit tunnel that leads out of New Street Station and North towards Crewe where we would change trains for the boat train. It soon became apparent why Birmingham and its surrounding conurbation earned its reputation for being the industrial heart of the nation. Looking out the carriage window, you could smell and taste unpleasant horrible acrid smells of second-hand factory smoke with factory after factory belching out spiralling curly grey smoke. This scenery would continue for about twenty-five minutes. Once we had passed through Wolverhampton, the landscape became more pleasing to the eye. Every year one of us would be given the job of the lookout, meaning keeping an eye out for the ticket collector. Experience had taught the weary travellers that the ticket collector would walk through the carriage at approximately forty-five minutes into the journey. It was about that time Mrs. O'Rourke would tell two of us to disappear into the toilet or move further up the train. The ticket collector would ask Mrs. O'Rourke how many passengers were traveling with her today. To which she would respond with a figure, which, of course was two less than the accurate figure.

With the ticket collector episode behind us, it was time for both myself and Mrs O'Rourke son to find a concealed spot where we could both have a cigarette. If Mrs O'Rourke found the two of us smoking, we would have been thrashed to within an inch of our lives and made to say the Rosary every day of the holiday. The best smoker's area was the area between the carriages where the door had a leather strap which enabled the window to partially open. Only when you had adjusted the buckle hole on the strap, you could fully open the window, which slid downwards. Upon reaching Crewe, we would all disembark and wait thirty minutes for the boat train to arrive. The boat train from Crewe to Holyhead was always a slower train than the first train. Thus, enabling the passengers, a better experience of scenic North Wales bringing a sense of wellbeing with the lush scenery on the one side and the coastal view on the other.

We all knew from sailing the Irish sea that the next part of the journey was the most daunting. Crossing the Irish sea was, at any time no joke. Two ships ferried passengers from Holyhead to Dun Laoghaire harbour. Princess Maude was the smaller of two and was used to carry cattle in WWII. The Hibernia transported troops only. With Britain being near bankruptcy after WWII it was decided not to scrap both ships which was most annoying to those who sailed on them. We learned at school that the Germans had a lot to answer for. My biggest complaint against the Germans was, why, didn't the bastards torpedo Princess Maude and Hibernia and have done with them? Had they torpedoed both of those rotting pieces of metal then the crossing to Ireland would have been for more enjoyable. On some occasions when the swell was high, you could spend half the voyage leaning over the ships railings and the other half giving the Irish sea the technicolour complexion. Sometimes the journey would take three hours, other times it could take up to six hours. There was a story circulating that on one particular voyage the sea was so rough the ship's captain wanted to return to harbour but was unable to turn the ship around because he feared it would capsize. My mother insisted that the crossing, the sea air, and the stiff breeze would prepare us for what lay ahead. Which was, in reality, a healthy farm life in the west of Ireland for the next six to seven weeks.

The intermittent light of a lighthouse or the sight of a port in a storm is the most welcoming sight a weary traveller can experience thus, walking down the narrow walkway from the ship and on to Dun Laoghaire port piled concrete platform was joyful for a dizzy young passenger. The boat train was always waiting to transport the boat's passenger, but, for some reason, it seemed to take an inordinate length of time. The train journey from the Dun Laoghaire to the Westland Row railway station in the centre of Dublin was short. There a meal would be ordered for all of us at a restaurant opposite the station. This meal needed to be quickly consumed because the train would soon be arriving to take us on the five-hour journey to County Mayo in the West. The first sense you experience when visiting the shores of the green isle is the beautiful smell of burning turf. I have never smelt an aroma like it outside Ireland. It has a non-aggressive aroma and it's pleasing to the nostrils - a far cry from the smells of burning coal.

The train journey to the west provides an excellent opportunity to understand why they call Ireland the emerald isle and why the British after being cordially invited as guests by the Irish into Ireland decided to stay and bring their baggage with them.

The wealth of Ireland is spread around its capital much the same as London is in the UK. The further away you travel the less money influences the inhabitants. The town of Athlone lies equidistantly between Dublin and Castlebar and is adorned by the tranquillity of the River Shannon. The second stage of the train journey gives way to tiredness and naps with long stares through the carriage window. Seeing white washed heavy-walled cottages supporting thickly thatched roofs and the small casement sash timber windows; men fishing in lakes and meandering rivers; endless green and burned heather surrounding well-stacked sods of turf waiting to be collected by a reluctant tireless donkey and his trailing cart. By the time we reached Castlebar, the day light had changed to darkness and we looked forward to disembarking. There waiting at the station would be Dad's sister Aunty Nancy. With her husband Jack and six children, they lived on an estate made up of a single row of houses situated on the Westport road heading towards Westport and eventually on to the beautiful island of Achill. This is where the north Atlantic rugged coastline could be viewed with its' high cliffs, small beaches that allow the ocean breakers to crash relentlessly.

Through tired eyes, we would say our goodbyes to our accompanying fellow passengers, the O'Rourke's.

Aunty Nancy would greet us with the word's

"Cead Mile Failte"

Meaning a thousand welcomes in Gaelic. I don't know, to this day, how my poor aunty Nancy and uncle Jack managed to accommodate us all that first night. Cousins would double up in bed or sleep at neighbours. Only then would the adults settle down and catch up with all the news from over the water in exchange for the local gossip in Castlebar. With breakfast finished it was time to walk down to the town before we were driven out to the Grandma McEvilly's farm in Plovervale not far from the village of Turlough and it's striking round Tower. The first few days living on the farm were the most challenging. At first, we would ask Grandma, where was the toilet? to which she would answer.

"Go and walk for twenty metres towards that high hedge running adjacent to the barn and make a name for yourself."

The daily task of fetching the drinking water was via walking across a field for thirty metres with a stainless-steel bucket until you reached a windbreak formed by a plantation of trees. Water from the spring had a beautiful pure natural taste, the kind of taste folk would give a small fortune for every day of the week. Being able to control a light with ease of a light switch was substituted with a lamp fuelled by paraffin and linen cloth.

Uncle Parky performed daily milking of cows. It was not wise to venture into the cow shed while milking was taking place as a few quick quirks of warm cows' milk into your face would ensure you didn't repeat that error.

CHAPTER 4 :
FARMING LIFE

The majority of the fowl and wildlife was alien to me when staying at the farm. Birds of all colours and size some with long beaks some with small beaks would fly in formation or flocks like good mates. During the haymaking months, species of various birds populated the skies with diverse species not known to city types. Their identity and names were only possible when the experience farming relatives and their neighbours chipped in. I was eternally grateful to my relatives and neighbouring farmers for educating me when it came to identifying the various bird species. Birds such as the Shoveler, Wigeon and Teal common together, with the Golden plover, Lapwing, Whooper swan, even the Peregrine. These birds I was informed would travel from Lough Conn near Crossmolina to Carrownmore Lough and, other loughs such as Lannagh located at the Town of Castlebar. I was an ill-informed youth from the city instantly pronging any trespassing, overweight, croaking frog whenever they crossed my path. I knew so little of the rustic world only, the world of urban life, which was the artificial world of automation and creeping plastic domination.

Around the immediate footprint of the farmhouse you could count, with a struggle, the total contingent of Grandma's army of clucking, gobbling and quacking fowl. Her platoon ranged from forty to sixty, comprising mostly of hens and chickens with the remainder being roosters, ducks, geese and turkeys depending on the necessary kill rate. Any fowl that were not performing or laying eggs walked a very tight rope that ended at the dinner plate.I became close to most of the fowl over the summer holidays. Nearly every morning, Grandma would despatch me to the hen house to find newly laid warm eggs. Failure to find eggs in the hen house would mean seeking alternative beds such as the barn or another outbuilding. Luckily, I always found enough eggs so we could have a couple of boiled eggs each with toast or scrambled eggs on toast. I always kept away from the large eggs because I hated duck and turkey eggs. Fortunately they were as rare as hen's teeth. She would spread homemade buttermilk all over the homemade white bread and the fire toasted bread. I did my level headed best not to eat the butter because it tasted very salty, and unlike the commercial butter we had in Birmingham. The milk was always warm because it was in a closed stainless-steel container. This was far better than the milk mother sometimes used when she ran out of fresh milk back in Birmingham. This milk tasted horrible because it had been subjected to a heating process before bottling. Sterilised milk, as it was known, which was a spin-off from WWII.

The rest of the food for lunch and supper was purchased from 'Paddy Moriarty's mobile grocery van' that parked itself at the bottom of the narrow front road leading from the farmhouse. It would take her circa fifteen mins to walk the distance and when we offered to walk it for her, she would hear none of it. When she arrived in to see what was in the van, she would climb up the steps and point her stick to identify what she wanted exactly. Meanwhile, she would be giving out with immense gusto what she thought of Moriarty's prices and his limited selection. She would be there inside that van for ages. I suppose this was her means of gleaning all the information and gossip in and around Plovervale and Breaffy farms. She had no interest in Castlebar because aunty Nancy in Castlebar was her spy there. During every visit she made to the van I made a point of tugging her skirt gently, to remind her to buy two jars of jam.

Grandma bought meats like sausages, bacon rashers, ham and

chunks of bacon to boil because she didn't like keeping pigs – who would! I suppose steak and beef were expensive and difficult to digest. Her shopping list, contained tea from China. China tea was different from India tea because Chinese tea leaves were far larger when dried but, weaker when brewed, so it seemed. We drank India tea in Birmingham. Chocolate and sweets were out of the question, but she'd buy us biscuits called 'Kimberley'. It was a great shame it was not possible to purchase them back in Birmingham. No need to buy any vegetables because she had a garden of veg that could have fed Napoleon's army on its retreat from Moscow. Strange but I do not remember being sick during any of the summer holidays stays with her. Perhaps it was the simple diet, fresh air and the exercise or moreover the Guinness.

One day she caught me looking at the farmyard fowl in a perplexed way, so she gave me a lecture on the differences between hens and chickens and the differences between a cockerel and a pullet. She went on to tell me that her Turkeys were European because they had ugly skin hanging from their beaks - unlike their cousins in American. The hens would only lay eggs for a maximum duration of three years after that they were only suitable for eating. Hens spent most of the day dust bathing, perching, foraging and preening. When they were performing, they would go quiet and then go missing into the barn or hen house. I was advised to keep an eye out for the brown hens because they laid brown eggs but could be aggressive. The other Hens laid only white eggs. These noisy farmyard creatures together with her three dogs and the ass tied up in the vegetable garden down at the bottom of the hill, were Grandma's extended second little family. A Rooster's cry of cock-a-doodle-doo replaced the mechanical alarm clock, which can let you down either with a battery issue or mechanical failure. The farm alarm never fails you when those fellows are around.

Most mornings Grandma would walk from the back door of the farmhouse to the centre of the yard with a bucket of feed to sprinkle amongst the fowl and invariably one or two tardy hens or slow ducks would stand in her way and nearly trip her up. This incident would bring about an instant display of Irish temper.

"Get out, yeah dirty little tings. agrow!"

"Lord Jesus, today and tonight. Isn't it shocking?"

After which, she would thrust her right foot in the general direction of the guilty fowl. I never knew a morning when this didn't happen. The incident repeated itself daily inside the farmhouse when the dogs got in her way as she walked from the kitchen table to the open hearth. Only this time she would be more accurate with her kick. The rules regarding farm behaviour, which include gates, are cast in stone – all gates needed closing at all times. If you find a farm gate open then close it and, find out why it was left open, or who opened it and forgot to close it. Leaving farmyard gates open can lead you to bankruptcy. Now again, tales of cattle rustling circulate, but fortunately, Plovervale and Breaffy farming fraternity were tightly knitted communities, so thieves did not prosper.

Dogs can be an asset to the farm or can be a significant liability. A dog out of control can run after the cattle causing them to panic and fall. Every cow is an integral part of the farm's livestock asset. No Insurance company will cover the risk of uncontrolled dogs. Grandma's instruction was to carry a dog lead at all times when walking through the fields in the event you walked into a field containing cattle. Although a stick can be a deterrent to the unruly dog, a lead is far more effective.

CHAPTER 4 :
HAYMAKING

Haymaking on the McEvilly farm was no different from any other farm in the Breaffy area. It involved the farmers sharing each other workloads which meant bringing together of families and neighbours. The initial process necessitates the cutting of ripe hay with a scythe during June. The scythe consists of a long handle with a large sharp edge used for cutting the mature hay into swaths. Once the grass was left to dry for a couple of weeks, it is time to turn it over for drying. Once dried, it will then be then shaken out and made into Cocini or Cutyeens. Once the Cocini was dry, it was shaken for a second time and gathered together finally to construct a haycock.

A substantial haycock could measure around ten to twelve feet high and should receive securing with the aid of 'sugans' or 'hay ropes' twisted and drawn over the stacks, then secured with heavy stone weights that would protect against potential strong winds. The farmer would 'head' the stacks by racking all the loose hay from the top to tidy it with the aid of a pitchfork and place loose hay back. The haystacks would stand in the field for circa one month and would then transport back to the haggard – traditional storage area for crops. The means of transporting the hay to the haggard was invariably an ass plus cart. As the years went by the means of transportation progressed to mean the introduction of low flatbed trailers and tractors. Although we had good fun in many ways, the youngsters worked hard and appreciated the value of hard physical work and its rewards. I often thought of those poor friends stuck in Sparkbrook for the summer months amidst the diesel fumes smoky chimneys and cramped conditions. We entertained ourselves hiding in the hays stacks to avoid work and jumping between the tractor and the rope dragging the haystack. We were too young to see the danger in that, but it was mighty craic so long as the tractor driver didn't see our antics and inform on us to our parents.Workers would take a short lunch break as the adage goes. 'Make hay while the sun shines' was always referred. Working late was rewarded with plenty of food and drink. Including bottles of the Guinness to make sure our energy levels were maintained.

Raiding Grandma's cupboards for fishing tackle after the harvest was an annual affair. The majority of the fishing rods would be standing idle from the year before. Not all the rods were workable, and it was necessary to prepare more rods by cutting down a branch from one of the trees within the windbreak plantation. Then we would whittle it into the shape of a rod and purchase fishing lines from the hardware store in Turlough village. We would go fishing without a permit in the Castlebar and Manulla Rivers. The rivers were always lush with fish because it seems nobody else bothered fishing. I suppose familiarity breeds contempt. Grandma was always grateful when we brought our fish home. We were certainly not the type of fishing enthusiasts who thought it was noble to throw their catch back into the river. We thought taking the fish home to her was always the right thing to do! Due to our limited city fishing skills we were only able to name some of the fish caught like, pike, trout, carp, or muskellunge; the names of other fish species is where our resourceful uncles came in useful once again - We must have appeared to have been complete philistines. The opportunity to fish in Sparkbrook did not exist. The bus fare out to Earlswood lakes, outside the city, was unaffordable and fishing in the public park pond in Small Heath park was not serious fishing in comparison.

CHAPTER 4 : THE COW IS CALVING

On a very early morning Grandma McEvilly came bursting through the back door and walked over to the uncles' bedroom door and banged on it in rapid succession. She shouted.

"The heifer is calving get up yeah pair of useless latchico's, get up out of bed and go down the field and help the poor cow! Lord! Isn't it shocking today and tonight, two fine men above in the beds and the poor cow is calving!!"

Uncle John was the first to make a move on himself. She said later that John looked like he levitated from his bed in an ascension type fashion. Before his feet had touched the bedroom floorboards, he had already taken off his trouser pyjama and had one leg in his corduroy trousers. My other Uncle Parky followed with similar gymnastics, and within a matter of four minutes, both strutted out of the farmhouse back door pulling up their unfastened trouser with braises trailing behind them. Wearing wellingtons both walked briskly down the steep hill in front of the farmhouse. jumped out of bed and dressed myself to see what all the fuss was about.

Grandma said to me "Where do yeah think you are off to Gasureen?"

"Off to see the cow calving, Grandma!"

"You'll do no such thing before yeah eat some breakfast at that table over there."

She had prepared breakfast for two before she realised my older brother Seamus's inquisitive nature had got the better of him and, as such, had walked down the field with John and Parky. I sat at the table and bolted down the standard two semi boiled eggs with two thick slices of farmhouse white bread suffocated with homemade buttermilk and a mug of teddy bear brown tea. Then without a thank you, I swivelled 180 degrees in my chair and jumped off the chair and ran straight out the back door and down the steep hill. By the time I had run down to the bottom of the hill with my belly full of breakfast I was in serious need of a rest and so decided to bend over and put my two hands on both my knees anf looked down making every effort not to looking down on brown substance my brother called heifers dust.When I raised my head after a few minutes of trying to recover my wind I saw five or six farmers walking and talking in two's behind a cow walking unsteadily with white stuff coming from its mouth. I asked my brother what was the problem with the cow. He told me that the cow was having a baby and, was not feeling so well, so it needed the attention of the uncles and neighbouring farmers.

After about an hour of waiting and watching a procession of farmers watching and trailing a labouring cow in distress, I became bored. I told my brother I was going to walk back to the farmhouse. To which he responded to watch out of for cow droppings spread around the field, as Grandma would not be happy should I walk in with that mess on my boots. I returned in the farmhouse to be greeted by Grandma and a Gaelic inquisition into the general well being of the latest potential asset to Plovervale farm. I told her as much as I knew as I could see a crate of small bottles of Guinness hidden under the table but no sign of minerals for likes of a Gasureen. After about an hour of reading superhero comics books and, another mug of teddy bears brown tea from a restless Grandma, my brother came bursting through the back door to tell us that the cow had calved and everything was all right. The relief on her face was like seeing somebody observe the sun rising for the first time. The aged and wrinkled skin peppered with freckles caused by excessive melanin and, multiple childbirths, and shaky hand morphed into a younger and happier woman.

Within seconds of hearing the good news, a small bottle of Guinness thrust itself into my hand. Initially, it tasted awful for first few slurps, but if you persevere at anything, one will become better at it - well that is what my mother always drilled into me - perfection achieved through repetition.

Within ten minutes, I was jumping the natural stream that fed the water well. If I jumped that stream once I jumped it a thousand times that afternoon. Then came hurdling practice for the Mayo Olympics where I bravely jumped like a hurdler going for the line. Superman dives over stoned dwarf walls stained with bird dropping which separated the all-important fields. Finally, Batman made an appearance when waging war on the criminals of Gotham City. We planned scrumping apples from neighbouring Welsh's orchard, but my brother said to me.

"It was time to report back to the house or search parties will be out looking!"

As we both approached the house, you could hear the craic was in full swing with violins and accordions blasting out feet tapping tunes: waltzes, four hand reals and other traditional music for quick step dances. When we entered the room from the back door, local farmers wearing their caps congratulated both my brother and I. The room was full of celebrating farmers sitting on hard wooden chairs positioned around the perimeter of the room. In the corner was a large wooden table with loads of gammon, pigs' feet, (Grubeens) a huge pot of unpeeled potatoes, white cabbage, ham, Jam, Irish Butter and thick slices of white bread. In attendance was farmer Quigley, our neighbouring farmer from over the hill just before Darrynanaff bog. Other neighbours joining were the Clarkes from just opposite the big field in front of Grandma's farmhouse. And, of course, the Kellys from Greeve who were relatives from Grandma's side. All had congregated in McEvilly's farmhouse to share in the celebration of new additional animal stock. Tumblers of Tullamore whisky and pints of Guinness together with the smoking of tobacco thumb stuffed thoroughly into white clay pipes and of course the holy water.

I was fifty per cent towards seeing the bottom of my second bottle of Guinness when the Batman performing episode and the Superman shenanigans began to take their toll, and the whole world started to cave in on me. Gingerly, I headed towards an unplanned siesta! The beast had finally been put to rest.

CHAPTER 4 : MY UNCLE PARKY

For years I would holiday in Ireland thinking Uncle Parky was a knowledgeable man because he could speak fluent Gaelic with ease. It was not for some time that I realised that he was tongue-tied and that the only person or persons who could understand him was his mother and the majority of the time his older brother John.Now and again, partially tongue-tied Uncle Parky would be instructed by his mother to take a heifer to the Friday cattle market at the Castlebar. Sometimes it was a heifer to be sold; otherwise, it was an older cow at the end of its milking life. Religiously, Grandma deliverd sleeping Parky an early morning bang on the bedroom door shouting get up you have a job to do today. Hapless Parky would have his breakfast and set off with a stick in hand walking the unsuspecting cow the six miles from Plovervale to Castlebar cattle market on his own. I often thought how dangerous it must have been walking a solo cow along the main tarmac road but Parky managed year after year. He would return home that night having had a few celebratory bottles of courage and tell my Grandma the latest gossip from the cattle market. The conversation between those two was fluent and with full eye contact.Those members of the family listening in from outside the inner circle would listen with frowned foreheads in silence to a conversation only a doting mother and a disadvantaged son would understand. When the opportunity arose for him to have professional help to improve his communication difficulties, his mother thought it was not such a good idea.

Parky, like most farmers, would always have an accompanying dog. His most loyal canine was a mixed breed called Di nun noon. He was a smart and didn't take long to train in the arts of behaviour when dealing with farm livestock. He was a permanent tail 'wagger' always eager to please at any moment of the day. One summer evening, poor Parky came into the farmhouse with tears running down his cheeks mumbling incoherently. Eventually, Grandma deciphered that his dog had consumed a mushroom containing poison, causing him to die slowly. Poor Parky had lost his only pal, his soul mate and was incandescent for a least a week. Coming from the city it was difficult to understand why a fully-grown man had become so close to an animal but really that little creature represented his inner happiness — something he could only express in words to those immediately close to him.Many years later, after his mother died at a good age, he decided to push his social boundaries. His new freedom meant he was able to visit the bars of Turlough, Ballavery and further afield to Ballina. He would have his fill of ale and at times mischievously ride his bike back to Plovervale with or without lights and to hell with the poilini sraidhaile.

One morning a commuter travelling to Castlebar noticed a bike on the side of the road lying in a bizarre position and decided to investigate. When he came alongside the bicycle, he saw an unconscious man lying prostrate in the ditch. This man turned out to be uncle Parky. Somebody had driven him off the road on his way home from his night out. His condition was serious, so an ambulance brought him to Castlebar hospital. Both legs had been mangled meaning both legs needed to be amputated. Then a strange thing happened, somebody or should I say some coward bought a brand-new bicycle and left it leaning against the front door of the McEvilly farmhouse. - somebody with a conscious. I visited uncle Parky in Castlebar Hospital. It was not a pleasant sight looking down on a man lying on his bed, suffering so much pain due to the actions of those unknow. The patient in the next bed asked.

"What time is it?"

To which Parky responded by answering with another question.

"Does it matter what time it is?"

I thought what a saddening way to end your days. Parky had lost his spirit, the very spirit that drove his inner strength against all that was against him. Parky lived for only several months after enduring several strokes.

CHAPTER 4 : THE CARNIVAL

Every year a travelling carnival visited Castlebar for two weeks during the summer. The carnival set itself up with the sweat and toil of its travelling crew and Castlebar locals. The centre of the town had a common green area called the Mall. It would remain there for two weeks. Like all travelling carnivals, it had the usual means of entertainment and the usual means of emptying the pockets of the local's hard-earned shillings. One year my cousin Sean and I decided to walk around the carnival to see if we could find any new attractions. After a while, we noticed changes to the revolving waltzes. The platform appeared to have been raised. Sean needed to investigate and climbed up into his seat. When I followed him into my seat, Sean gave me a dig into the ribs with his elbow.

"Look at that dirty thing! That's crafty, Finbarr O'Flaherty he is in charge of the horse racing roulette wheel. He just put his hand in his pocket to pull out his handkerchief, blew his nose, and then placed his handkerchief into his pocket with an accompanying Irish five-pound note!"

It was at that moment we realised that there was holiday money to be made. We decided to observe the antics of Mr O'Flaherty a little closer. The following night, we watched the workings of the locals operating the horse racing stall which meant working inside the stall and selling the tickets before the horse roulette wheel turned again and, of course, the antics of one Mr O'Flaherty. True to form, our previous observation proved to be correct. We also noticed that the wheel was not turning, as it ought to. Of the twenty-five horses' names shown on the revolving wheel, it appeared a small number of horses were winning far more frequently than others. We observed that this was inevitable because the wheel was rubbing against the supporting backplate just where the most popular horses scribed names were. There was one particular horse that seemed to win an awful lot more than all the other horses. After a lengthy discussion over strategy, I offered to work within the stall. By volunteering my services to sell the tickets, it would mean I'd be able to grab the tickets having the names of the most winning horses which I would sell to my cousin standing outside the stall. We carried out our little scam on a penultimate night as a trial, and it proved successful considering it was a quiet night. The following night was the last night when the town raffle would be drawn, pulling a large crowd. This event produced the most popular night of the two weeks before the carnivals' end.

At the end of the last night, we arranged to meet up in the ice cream parlour house called Cafola coffee house which incidentally was owned by an Italian who moved with his family from his home town in Sicily to set up an ice cream parlour and coffee house in Castlebar on the main street. We counted out the proceeds, and it amounted to sixty-eight Irish Pounds. Considering you could buy fifteen pints of Guinness for one Irish Pound this was a good night.

We spent the remainder of the holiday buying and smoking packets of Carolls's cigarettes in their twenties; visiting the cinema every night of the week; ordering large rounds of draft pints instead of bottles of Guinness. The owners of the carnival held an internal investigation because the takings were so small, considering it was the busiest night of the carnival in the middle of summer. Their findings were inconclusive. However, Mr O'Flaherty's services were no longer required. They tell you the house always wins but, on this occasion, it didn't!!

CHAPTER 4 : GOING TO KNOCK

It was a Saturday afternoon when both aunties Dolly and Ninny told me it was a good idea for me to accompany them to a place called Knock. I was young and gullible when I believed the older siblings that knock was a seaside resort on the Atlantic coast - Both aunties were getting on in life and gained comfort in religion.

We walked into the centre of Castle Bar with sandwiches, flasks of tea, bibles, Rosary beads and Holy water and waited for the bus to arrive. After about a ten-minute wait an old looking unwashed green single-decker bus arrived making a juddering sound with its brakes. About fifteen of us, mainly older women, embarked up the short stair of the bus and only upon the presentation of the correct bus ticket where we allowed to sit down on the hard tightly fitted leather seats with a rounded chrome perimeter and, away we went. The journey took longer than I thought it would. I asked auntie Dolly on more than one occasion where exactly was the village of Knock and she told me in no uncertain terms that it was on the way Claremorris and Ballina, which of course, meant absolutely nothing to me. Travelling there I noticed the roads were narrower because many were off the main drag. By the time we reached the village of Knock, I had eaten most of the sandwiches with two cups of flask tea.

As I stepped off the bus, I noticed that the vast expense of the

Atlantic Ocean was not in sight. All I could see was on the horizon were buildings washed with whitewash and the majority of people in the crowd were old and dressed in dark clothing and looked as if they had not seen the sun or the sea for years. They reminded me of creatures waking up after hibernation. Aunty Ninny asked me to follow her, which I did, only to find myself kneeling on a church bench. The church filled quickly with solemn-looking folk. Within three minutes, the Priest walked out of his presbytery, followed by three altar boys. One was not so young. Then came the mass of which forty minutes of listening to a Priest's forty minutes of slurring voice delivering a rambling epistle. The altar boy shook the bell, to ensure the congregation heard the ringing during stages of mass. Sometimes folk would stand, other times they would kneel on the bench and sit down whenever possible. I received a sharp dig into the ribs to remind me to walk down to altar rail to orally receive holy communion. I heard an awful lot about this man called Jesus through my headmasters rants every school assembly. The mass finally ended after ninety minutes and not a word of it I understood. Latin was not my favourite subject at school, nor, was it anybody else's, come to think about it. Perhaps this is karma for my antics at the carnival, or I hadn't said enough Hail Marys every night before I went to sleep.

We stood there waiting for the Priest to walk off the altar and return to the presbytery. Only then could the congregation vacate the church building the Priest and his acolytes decided against taking a right and veered left up the aisle and out through the church back doors. Worshippers to the front, rear and back of me followed the Priest like animals going into Noah's Ark. We trailed the procession for two hours looking like lost souls. In front of the procession was the acolyte carrying a horizontal cross with a little man nailed to it. I suppose the Priest pulled rank and didn't want to hold the wooden cross for any length of time and who would blame your holy grace the eejit. Anyway, the quadrophonic sound resonating in both my ears came from auntie Dolly and Ninny saying their prayers out loud. I mentioned to Aunt Ninny that I was feeling somewhat parched and was desperate for a drink of water from anywhere. I suggested it might be a good idea to dish the palms of my hands into the holy water bowl located at church rear entrance. She looked at me in a way only a deranged woman sitting on a broom and wearing a witch's hat would look at you. She responded to my suggestion by saying.

"Ah, will yea now? Ya, little gombeen!"

"I'll give you an awful skelping into the butt of ya lug if I hear anything like that again, agrow!!"

After that sobering little dressing down, I had learned my lesson. Dante's third circle was going to be challenging to pass through successfully! What followed were the Rosary consisting of loads of Hail Marys, and then one Our Father. After ten minutes, the Rosary had passed, and my thirst was nowhere near being quenched. After that came Benediction, which meant my nostrils were inhaling the smell of what I thought was Frankincense and Myrrh – well, so I thought. Just as well we were out in the open because back home in the local parish church, they always burn it on inside the church. I didn't know what was coming next? Was it going to be baptism? Possibly a marriage? Could there be an anointment perhaps even an ordination? Fortunately, not. After three hours the pilgrimage, if you can call it that, was over.

The return bus journey to Castlebar seemed a lot shorter, and the passengers appeared to be in good spirits. I thought to myself that the real sinners have had the burden of guilt lifted from their shoulders. The way some of them behaved on the return journey, you would swear they were latent serial killers.

CHAPTER 4 : CROAGH PATRICK (764M)

On the road to West Port traveling from Castlebar, you can see a little peak shaped mountain above the villages of Murrisk and Lecanvey on the left-hand side approximately eight miles before you reach Westport. It's called Croagh Patrick and nicknamed the reek by the locals. It is an important site of pilgrimage in Mayo. When you see it, it will remind you of your school days because it had the shape of a triangle. This mountain is famous amongst its local inhabitants around the west of Ireland. Its popular because of the Patron Saint of Ireland Saint Patrick walked up this mountain to say prays and starve himself, or should I say fasted for forty days and nights.

St Patrick's acts of penance led the way to thousands of pilgrims repeating the act every year when they walk up and down the mountain side, hoping that their acts of penance will allow them access to the stairwell to heaven. I earned my access to the stairwell to heaven when I attended Knock Shrine that fateful Sunday afternoon when kneeling on my knees for what seemed an eternity with Aunty Ninny and Dolly by my side. Several of my cousins in Castlebar proudly confess to climbing the Reek every year sometimes, in their bare feet. They would ask me to accompany them on their next pilgrimage to which I responded that the majority of my sins were venial, your sins must be mortal. Every year they would ask me to climb with them, so I eventually gave in mainly because I would be on my own again if they all went off to climb the Reek. Moreover, I was told there was a bar at the top of the mountain where I could congratulate myself after completing the climb. So off I went accompanied by my cousins on Reek Sunday, which is the last Sunday in July. It's the busiest day of the Reek year when twenty-five thousand people climb the mountain. I had and a clean pair of hiking boots, a flask of something and, a sandwich box strapped to my waist. On a clear day, we arrived at the bottom of the mountain where there are car parking spaces, toilets, and an information centre that sold or hired walking sticks. Because it was my first and hopefully, my last climb up this mountain, I bought a walking stick to assist my climb and to keep as a souvenir.

The first station is called Leacht Benain located at the base of the cone-shaped mountain. What they didn't tell me was it took five hours to walk or scale the mountain. My Castlebar relatives led me to believe that it is easy to walk because so many people complete it annually. However, I soon found out it is not quite like what they said it is. The first hour of the walk after the station is at a steep angle. My cousins were a lot fitter and had more stamina. Their smoking and drinking habits had no effects on their ability to walk up a steep incline, unlike my weak body.

Two of my cousins were walking in their bare feet seemingly without pain. Before you commence the climb, you will notice that there is a marble statue of Saint Patrick on the right-hand side positioned on top of a five feet high pillar. Built into the pillar is a box with opening in the shape of a slit and a sign above requesting donations for the maintenance of the church located at the top mountain. The first difficulty you encounter is slippery small rocks, boulders and pebbles rolling down the mountain. Loose rocks and small stones traveled down the mountain when people failed to gain there footing. The presence of shale in layers became difficult to negotiate at times and I slipped on more than one occassion. What surprised me was the profile of folk climbing the mountain. People from a broad church were out seeking to accomplish their ultimate annual reek goal so they could boast about it to their families and friends. My climb as far as I was concerned was a one-off to appease the relatives.

Ben Goram, on the western spur of the mountain, is reachable within three hours and more than half way up Croagh Patrick. Here at 559m up is a milestone identified by a small number of medium-sized stones heaped on top of each. The last section of the climb is the most challenging again because of the steepness and the wet loose rocks. The Second Station is at the summit, where you will find a chapel and a stone slab embedded into uncoursed angular stonework. The inscription on the slab informs you of the following:

A. Kneel and say, seven Our Fathers, Hail Marys and I creed;
B. Pray near the chapel for the pope's intentions;
C. Walk fifteen times around the chapel saying fifteens Our Fathers, fifteen Hail Marys;
D. Walk seven times around Leaba Phadraig saying seven Our Father, seven Hail Marys, and one creed.

I managed to do one our father and five Hail Marys because I had some dispensation coming my way for my efforts at the Knock shrine. The Cairn, at the side of the mountain on the way to the summit, is where you overlook Clew bay is breath taking. Tradition tells you that there are three hundred and sixty-five islands in the bay - One for every day of the year. The most commonly known bay of them all is Dura Island purchased in 1997 by John Lennon from Beatles.

I had walked the most walked mountain in Ireland but I could not find an ale house or a bar as promised by those terrible relatives. I did find a chapel and, another sign made of marble containing a message asking the general public to take their rubbish with them because there is no rubbish collection facility at the top of the mountain. Also, I found a Saint Patrick's bed, which is delineated by a horizontal single tubular handrail supported by four poles. Whatever remained of my lunch box and the drink I had in the flask was devoured at the top of the mountain. After communal prayers, we sat down on some large boulders and talked while we rested for around 45 minutes. I walked down the mountain at a faster pace than I walked up to it. I made sure that I kept to the stable path at all times walking off track was not an option at any time. It was dangerous because your feet could easily slide on the small loose stones.

The finish is situated at Roilig Muireis where you find another car park and facilities. The finding of gold on the mountain in the 1990s stirred high expectation of newfound wealth. Still, the potential newfound wealth equating to three hundred and sixty million Euros has never been realised because Mayo Environmental Group and the Mayo County Council decided not to allow mining and the gold has never been touched to this day. The gold and its potential betterment for those in and around the region of Mayo area will never be.

I was more than happy to sit in between of my cousins on the back seat of the car that evening. My legs were tired and my feet were painful. It doesn't take long to drive back to Castlebar during which, not a word was uttered. The welcomed silence on the way home gave me time to reflect on those before me who had walk the Reek; some in their bare feet; some carrying a heavy cross in the dark strong winds heavy rain and clouds. Perhaps faith and hope have a far greater latent force than I was led to believe by my primary school headmaster.

CHAPTER 4 : A DAY IN THE BOG

One Saturday morning, when I was lying in my kip, in Auntie Nancy's house, I heard her voice shouting up the stairs.

"Would anybody like to visit bog with uncle Jack?"

My older and shrewder siblings remained still in their beds, pretending to be dead. I thought for a while and said. 'Yes!' I would not mind going to the bog with Uncle Jack. I got dressed and ran downstairs.

"Go raibh maith agat fear og" (Well done young man),

She placed a flask of tea in a bag for the journey and a large circular can with a lid on it which was labelled 'Bog tea'. Another rectangular tin marked 'Bog food' was thrust into my midriff. Within minutes we were off in uncle Jack's Volkswagen towing an empty trailer ready to have my first ever day in the bog. Uncle Jack told me.

"The Bog is an Irishman's horizontal mine." He went on to say, "the Bog allows easy access and a cheap method to extracting winter fuel safely."

In comparison to the traditional British method, working the Bog is relatively safe, healthy and did not need for you to travels miles under the ground to work in unhealthy conditions. Sometimes, under a clear blue sky and an incoming Atlantic Ocean breeze. On the drive to the Bog, he further explained that 'Peat' was an Irishman's coal and that turf was cut vertically with what is known as a turf cutter or a sledge. The average depth of a Bog can be between three to five metres deep. They are formed over thousands of years when lakes fill with plant debris and sphagnum moss as well as other plants. The top layers of the Bog are not as compressed as the lower layers. Therefore, when the cutting takes place with a cutter removes about half meter horizontally and put to one side. This turf is used to start a fire or to keep a fire topped towards the end of the night. Upon completion of the removal of the top layer the cutter then has access to cut deeper veins of turf, which were richer and of denser material. The cutter would throw the deeper denser turf over his shoulder on to the bank this would then be loaded into a wooden wheelbarrow and transported some five to ten yards to a spread are and tipped. This cycle repeated until enough turf collected for the forthcoming winter was complete. The next stage is to stack the tipped turf in the spread area in a way all the sods are allowed turf to dry. They leave the stacks of turf for a week. It is then ready to turn over which generally happens in late April. Sometimes there can be a very wet May so the turf in stacked in a castling manner this means stacking sods like house bricks but with gaps to create a vent to help a draft. If all goes well weather-wise, it would not be necessary to return to the Bog until no earlier than June or no later than late July.

So here we were in the middle of July working on transporting the dried turf from the spread area out to the trailer parked on the access road to the bog. We loaded the cart, which was pulled by an ass borrowed for the day from one of uncle Jacks cronies. The poor ass, I felt so sorry for him. He had no union to protect him, nobody to negotiate his workers' rights or even pay rise. Now and again he would give out a loud bray that could be followed by an enormous, noisy, smelly fart notably when you guided him by holding his bridle to the access road, which was only thirty yards away. I suppose that was his way of telling you enough is enough. I imagined him saying.

"I know the way yeah plebe!! I have been doing this for the last

15 years on minimum pay."

The only silver lining for the unfortunate ass was that the turf was fifty per cent lighter when it dried out in time to take home. After three hours of graft, we sat down on a seat made up of stacked sods of turf. We ate lunch together during this time and I managed to look around only to see vast peatlands of the vast wilderness, where natures' water storage acted as a buffer against seasonal flooding and created a breeding ground for habitats for birds and plants. I remembered watching a TV programme entitled mother nature, which stated Bogs stored more carbon than all the forests in the world. The language I heard that day while working in the bog reminded me of the language I had listened to when I entered the lodger's room in 3 Palmerston road Sparkbrook.

"How is she cutting? Throw it well back to the makers Name?"

Sometimes when the ass was not performing his duties well enough or, when one of us managed to steer the cart into the soft ground causing it to sink up to its axle. Uncle Jack would shout out.

"Go on yeah filthy article, yeah gobshite of a thing, agro, shagging latchico, good man yourself, go on yeah fecking blaggard."

I did feel sorry for the cursed ass him, but he was well accustomed to such verbal abuse.

That afternoon we carried out the same number of loads to the trailer. We loaded the trailer up an off we went, myself rubbing my eyes not necessarily from tiredness but more from airborne flaky dried peat that had detached itself from the dried sods of turf. This was not a common irritant to those working in the bog year after year but, but very common for city boys. I was rubbing my eyes for what seemed to be for weeks afterwards. When I entered auntie Nancy's house with uncle Jack that evening, the crafty cousins and siblings, said I had a real sower puss on me.

"Hardly surprising" I responded, "Considering I was the only young worker of any value in the house!"

The following day, during the many protracted eye-rubbing sessions, I mentioned to Sean, that Jack, although strong in his long silences, gave me the impression that he didn't like me for whatever reason. Sean told me that my accent reminded him of the time of his internment without trial for six years. I was shocked indeed, very shocked upon hearing this information and, I asked Sean.

"What the hell are you talking about, ya eejit. Had uncle Jack committed murder or robbed a bank?"

"No such thing, agrow." bleated, my cousin,

He went on to say during the struggles of the 1920s The majority of Irish citizens wanted Ireland to be a free of the shackles of the British empire and become a Republic. Many people, indeed the vast majority of Protestants with loyalist tendencies thought the opposite to this idea and considered that course of action would be the start of the breakup of the British empire and would, therefore, do anything within their power to prevent it. The loyalists hell-bent on avoiding a civil war on the Island of Ireland started rounding up all the folk they imagined would weaponise a civil war. Men like blacksmiths who could make guns or swords and de-mob soldiers returning home from overseas conflicts cause by the ever-expanding British Empire. Uncle Jacks father fell under the heading of a Blacksmith. But the authorities could not find your man, so they interned Jack.

His internment lasted for six years for no apparent reason, other than he was Jack Senior' son. Incarcerated without cause and without charge. This meant he was in the wrong place at the wrong time as so often is the case when troubles erupt between the people on the two little islands off the continental shelf of Europe. During the time of his internment, he managed to build a two-foot-high statue of the holy cross made of the discarded matches from fellow internees some, much older prison inmates. Jack was only sixteen at the time and was twenty-two years of age when released from internment.

CHAPTER 5 :
ATKINSONS

I t was never made apparent to us as a family why my mother had two birthdays. Mom never had time to explain many things in life to us because she was too busy raising a large family. We, therefore, always celebrated her two birthdays.She agreed to explain the mystery of two birthdays as she got older. In the early part of the 20th century in Mayo, and, in other more impoverished rural regions of the west of Ireland, a birth officially is recorded at the local post office. However, many folks for whatever reason be it, the cold weather or poor health sometimes delayed to the post office to record the birth many weeks after the event. My mother christened Mary Kate Atkinson, was born with one green and one brown eye, the second child of four children born within the marriage of Nora Flynn and Willian Atkinson in a thatched cottage located between Ballyvary and Straide. Ballyvary was a one-horse town circa six miles from Castlebar. Castlebar was second largest town in County Mayo after Ballina. She had one older brother called Joseph Martin, one younger brother called William Joseph and one younger sister named Delia.

She was born into poverty in a small, heavily thatched house with one large room, which served as a living room and kitchen with an open grange fireplace including an adjoining bedroom where everybody slept. There was a twenty-year gap between her eldest brother and her youngest sister. The school she attended was a single building and housed children of all ages up to the age of thirteen and was intrinsically not there for academics in life but more for the next generation having more and greater survival skills. My mother did not walk to school in her bare feet, but many did! Her education, whatever she had, provided her with the ability to read and write, giving her essentially, the three Rs. The problem was all children needed teaching in the Irish language, which created a problem because the first language spoken throughout the newly formed free state was English due to British imperialism. Schooling in two different languages must have been a real wrench. I am sure the disruption and frustration of being taught subjects by another man's language created an existential crisis solvable only by seeking divine intervention, which, of course, was the church through the communication of a Latin.

The people of Ireland invited the British to Ireland and by the time the people of Ireland asked the British to leave the Island of Ireland in 1916, some eight hundred years later. Except for the Northern six counties, which remain under British rule to this very day. The indigenous speakers of Irish suffered persecution during the British residence resulting in the Gaelic language losing its popularity and intellectual property.

The Atkinson homestead was like most homesteads housing large Catholic families and was considered too small to support two adults and four children. It, therefore, fell upon my Grandfather to travel to England in search of work. Unfortunately, the great depression did not pass by the Irish republic nor the United Kingdom and his search for betterment was not successful. Weeks, months and years would pass without remittance. The Atkinson family did what most families did during those times of severe hardship; they survived the difficulty on a meagre, diet, with very few surprises especially around Christmas time and of course good single parentage. One event that did manage to keep spirits high would be the visits to the next village for the Ceilidh. A Ceilidh was a gathering of the clans for entertainment held in one of the local villagers living rooms.

The lining of wooden farm chairs contouring the perimeter of the room created a dance area. Once the music started and the holy water extracted from the tabernacle, it was the turn of the self- acclaimed five clans of Connaught namely the Burkes, the McNicholas', the Stanton's, the McEvilly's of course, the Gallagher's with affiliated members, the Devaney's. The sounds of fiddles, flutes, whistles, harps, banjo accordions and bodhram with beater. Irish traditional music blasting far afield. Dance music made up of the reel, the jig, the hornpipe, four hand reals, with young members of the village, those with attitude (fear og treallusach)) dancing quick steps in time to the music. Fervent blasting of Irish music would continue into the early hours of the morning. Stories and tales told by at least one member from each family. The holy water would be flowing, and with one eye on the emptying bowl of holy water and the other on the lookout for the local's police (Poilini an tsradbhaile) a man with failing memory and a faltering voice would be heard delivering a recitation in the mother tongue. Grandma Nora Atkinson was one of five sisters who had planned to escape the island of Ireland and its suppressed history to immigrate to the land of opportunity called America. Between all five Flynn sisters, they managed to save and to pay for the passage to the land of opportunity. A week before they were to set sail, they attended a dance in the local village hall of Turlough so as the young ladies could bid their farewells to their friends and neighbour.

It was during that dance that Nora Flynn took a shine to a young man called William Atkinson so much so that she decided not to go to America with her sisters and to see how the land lay over the next few months. This ill-fated meeting between Nora and William blossomed in to love, and both were married soon afternoon. What followed was a life of hardship for the stay at home Nora while her sisters experienced a better life in America. One particular sister married well and managed to raise and educate two children, both of whom are lawyers in Chicago. It was my understanding that the remittance of spare monies was necessary to help the younger sister whenever matters became unbearable. My mother received several letters from a Judge in America during the 1950s, which she would read to us when we were children. The reading of letters from America by Mom to us had little significance. However, as time passes, you do learn to appreciate the importance of any supporting communication.

CHAPTER 5 :
UNCLE JOE

One Friday evening, when the Atlantic prevailing wind and its accompanying drizzle pelted the small windows of the Atkinson cottage, a knock came from the upper part of the cottage front door. Nora Atkinson opened the door cautiously , and there stood William Atkinson standing there dripping wet and tired after a long train and boat journey from Birmingham. He had returned with a promise that he would stay a month but, as it turned out, it was a week. The reunion, although short, brought a week's happiness with neighbours visiting and asking questions about England and was it worth leaving Ireland. Having the presence of their father around meant a great deal to Joseph, Mom, Delia and Willie Joe. William senior presence brought a sense of completeness together with security.

My mother's memories of that week were vivid. She remembers well the moment she was up in the field, reaping the harvest with her mother and sister and, while straightening her back and wiping sweat from her brow she noticed seeing her father William walking up to the road towards Ballyvary station with her older brother Joseph walking alongside him carrying two suitcases. In reality, her father was abducting Joe and taking him to England at the grand age of thirteen. Although Joe was tall and strong looking for his age, he had a very young and innocent mind and knew very little of the outside world. Furthermore, his lack of education as a result of him being kept at home to help his mother would have been a considerable hindrance to his future well being. William's selfish act was to have a devastating impact on his two daughters' and young son. Joe's absence meant there was no male around the house to protect the girls or young willie-joe. Joseph's youth and strength was imperative with the harvest and the cutting and gathering of turf from the bog to the outhouse for the winter months. With Joe around, there was hope for a future in Ireland. There was no hope if he went to England and never sent any monies back.

Uncle Joe travelled to England on a lie and a promise. Firstly, his father lied to him when he told him he was going to England to see his relatives and, secondly, his father promised he would shortly return home to see his mother. He did see his mother again after seventeen years. The reasons for Williams actions were never fully understood by the rest of the family. It will never be known, why he sent his thirteen-year of age semi-literate son to work in the cellar of a public house called the Wheatsheaf in Sheldon, in the South of Birmingham. Which is still there to this day although, it has received numerous re-furbishments. Joe was young, innocent and vulnerable. He later informed his nieces and nephews that working in a beer cellar became so unbearable, that he likened it to being in a dungeon. After a year of being subjected to ongoing verbal abuse, persistently referred to as being a 'Duck egg', 'Thick mick', 'Red neck' 'Stupid paddy' and being paid shockingly meager money for long hours convinced Joe that he needed to be accepted into this harsh belligerent British society and learn to assimilate.

So, at the age of fourteen, Joe lied his way into the British army, which enabled him to escape the bullying and poverty. Joe's first British army posting was in India. It lasted the best part of a decade during which time he acquired a Birmingham accent from his fellow soldiers which made him indistinguishable. I remember Uncle Joe telling my mother upon his return from India that, it was tradition for an Indian father to remain in bed for seven days to celebrate the birth of his son. My mother considered this as being too much information and became incandescent with rage and resentment.

CHAPTER 5 :
AUNTIE DELIA

Six months after we relocated to Hall Green we decided to treat Mom for a nice meal at the favourite her restaurant to show our appreciation for all the hard work she had done us. It was during the meal she talked about her earlier life.

She said, "Life hasn't been easy, not like it is now."

She and her younger sister left Ireland because they had seen more dinner times than dinners. My sister asked her why she insisted on the grandchildren having dolls and prams. She said it was because both she and her sister Delia never had toys when they were children. Their father found it difficult remit monies. It was, therefore, only a matter of time that they too would need to travel to find work out of necessity and the only choice being England.

So, at a young age, they both headed off to Birmingham, the same town their brother Joseph had initially moved to.My mother told me that she managed to get a job as a live-in barmaid in a Public House.One night she told me, she was relaxing in on her night off in her bedroom above the bar when she noticed the doorknob slowly turning. On the other side of the door was a Welsh man attempting to force his way into her bedroom to have his way. She was so terrified; she screamed and screamed until the customers ran up the stairs and handed out a good beating.I often wondered why Mom always told us when we were younger.

"Never trust a welsh man!!"

She didn't remain in that occupation for much longer after that and went to work at the British Small Arms factory located at Small Heath Birmingham during the peak of the blitz. During the Second World War, the Germans had been successful in bombing the factory. The BSA factory was an essential target for them because it made more than half the guns used in the WW2. Mom told me that she stood outside the gates of the factory the morning after the bombing blitz 19-20 November 1940 when four hundred tonnes of high explosives were dropped killing 53 workers and injuring hundreds more. Many of the night shift stayed at their benches due to tiredness instead of running to the bomb shelter. Before the day shift started, a man stood on steps shouting through a handheld cone-shaped loudspeaker.

"Do not to look down when walking to your place of work."

There was no time to remove the bodies so, 'Quick lime' was spread around as a temporary measure. What she heard next stayed with my mother all her life - the man shouted.

"Hitler is coming, and he is coming for you!!"

My mother never mentioned her experiences during the war. This made me a belatedly angry and, I asked,

"Why did you travel to England? You knew the British were at war with Germany!! You could have gone back to Ireland anytime; it was neutral the same as Switzerland?"

She responded by saying they had nothing, like so many Irish that came over.

"We were all economic refugees!!"

Delia, Mom's younger sister, was, according to her, 'Too pretty to be smart!' Mom being the older and more able of the two sisters always needed to look out for Delia. Her sister had many assets; However, Delia's most striking asset was her beauty and her youthful looks together with her colleen complexion and her natural rouge meant she was stunner. She was very popular when she attended the Moseley Irish arranged and managed by O' Gallahan. She was the reason Mom and Dad met at the dances in the first place. When Dad was single and out 'trapping', he ventured to the Tower Ballroom in Edgbaston because he had heard there was a beautiful young colleen from Ballavary called Delia attending. Ballavary, which was not far from Plovervale, would mean that Delia would be a 'Towney' and they would have plenty of things in common. Legend has it that Dad walked up and down the line looking for pretty young women from Mayo, building up enough courage to cross the bar rail and ask her out for a dance. He searched, and he searched and searched, and while rubbing shoulders with other candidates, he noticed my mother and asked her if her name was Delia.

Mom said. "No! It's not!"

"Arah" said Dad, "You will do!!"

Many men had passed my mother to ask Delia for a dance but, one man did not want to that night. That was Dad, his name was James McEvilly from Plovervale near Castlebar.

When my mother and father started courting, they would go to the Irish dances in Moseley every Saturday night to meet up with the other Irish in the city. Most of who were living in areas as far as Erdington in the North of the city. The organiser of the dances Mr O'Gallahan would always ask my Dad to put a good word in for him when he was talking to Delia because he took a fancy to her and he would tell my Dad that one day he was going to be a rich man. My Dad would pass the word on, but Delia had her own idea of her perfect man and like many folks in those days who were lucky to be alive having survived the war, money was not important.Indeed, not that important that you would need to go out with somebody for their money and not because you liked them. Delia did meet a man of her dreams, and his name was Harry. He was younger than her was but better educated. Harry gained such high scores when sitting the Irish leaving certificate examination which meant the way would be paved for him to study medicine or law. He chose instead like a lot of Irishmen to cross the Irish Sea to England for the bright city lights and the prospect of employment with a future which he obviously could not see happening in a depressed town of Claremorris. Harry and Delia got married the same time Mom and Dad relocated from Edgbaston to Sparkbrook. My parents had an arrangement that Mom's newlywed sister could move into the house they had vacated. It could not have been a solid start to the marriage, moving into that level of poverty to remain in England just for work.Harry, like most immigrants arriving in the UK, was unable to find employment commensurate with his level of education and could not find a job other than an industrial painter. So, he went to work painting factories.

One day Delia received a message to say that Harry had fallen off scaffolding and taken to the hospital in an ambulance. It turned out he has broken both his ankles and legs falling through scaffolding boards and hitting the ground below. So severely broken was his bones that he could not walk for six months and did not return to full employment for two years. The accident brought about great hardship for both Delia and Harry and their five young children. The much need for family allowance was a godsend - one of the perks of living in England and its then socialist sense of fairness. One day Delia sent her eldest son Kevin to pick up the family allowance from the post office. Kevin at that time had a friend who was older and bigger. He had befriended him earlier, and his friend's background was not obvious when perhaps it should have been. The only detail they had was that his name was Johnny O'Malley. He asked if he could accompany Kevin to the post office. When Kevin returned home, his mother asked him for the allowance money. Poor Kevin was unable to find it and was at a loss as to where it might have disappeared. Johnny, of course, had little knowledge of its whereabouts and soon became a persona non grata.

My Dad helped out over the two years as you would expect an

extended immigrant family to do. Harry's employer told him that he had a slim chance of being awarded any form of compensation. Upon hearing this, my Dad went into a rage and made an appointment with an Irish solicitor. He was told he had a good case for a claim based on negligence of both main contractor and subcontractor.

Two years after the accident, Harry received nearly nine thousand pounds in compensation. The judge decided unwisely to remit the money to Harry as a lump sum amount, whereas he should have awarded the money over some time in a structured fashion. Which would have meant Harry slowly becoming familiar with the valued of cash. As it turned out, Harry misspent the money and was broke just after two years. During which time the family moved to Solihull then back to Acock's Green.

CHAPTER 5 : COUSINS

During the school Summer and Easter holidays, while uncle Harry was in recovering from his broken bones, I would stay with Delia's house in Edgbaston. I always spent my time with my cousin Kevin. He was older than me more intelligent and streetwise. I suppose when you endure poverty and hardship as they had to your mind becomes more focused. We took advantage of having more freedom to get up to more mischief when I was with Kevin. Sometimes we would walk into the city centre to have a look at the huge department stores.Then on the way home return a different way. Instead of walking the long sensible way up the alleyway, we would take a short cut and approach the alley from the north, which meant climbing over the parapet wall located on top of the retaining wall to the side of aunties house. We then free dropped down a large wall six to eight feet high on to Auntie Delia's roof ridge tiles, then sliding down the pitched roof tiles until the eaves guttering allowed us to stop.

Finally, sliding down the rainwater pipe to safty on the ground. Kevin made it look easy, but I was always scared and excited not enough to fill my pants but enough to do again and again. Whatever questions I asked him he always had an answer. One day I asked him why was it his nose was still running, and he said he didn't know other than he had had a runny nose for four years. I suppose I should not have asked the question. The real answer was poverty and deplorable living conditions. Whatever difficulties he encountered him, he never allowed them to grind him down.

During some of the summer weeks, Kevin would come and stay with us in Sparkbrook. We more or less got up to the same mischief, like sneaking back in through the back door of the Waldorf picture house or sneaking into the Embassy Sports-drome double fire escape door when the lights were down prior to the start of the wrestling. One time we had an ice-cream fight at the rear of the Embassy using thrown out, contaminated ice cream as ammunition. On another day we were mucking around on one of Dad's jobs nearing completion. We thought it would be good fun to throw wet cement on the heads of innocent unsuspecting pedestrians from the first floor. The last time we did it, Kieron threw a lump of wet cement deliberately on to a bald man's head landing with pinpoint accuracy. Kevin thought this was hilarious until he jumped off the chair and landed into a bucket of water - perhaps the joke was on Kevin. The unfortunate victim made a vociferous complaint to my Dad about the amount of rubbish falling off the building. My Dad could not understand what all the fuss was about as it was not different from any other site he had constructed. We kept a low profile for some time after that little incident.

One Saturday morning, we were sitting and rotating forwards on the horizontal bars that formed the bus stop for the nr 13. The very bus stop I was forced to look at Mrs Meehan' s face every school morning. Our curiosity got the better of us, and we thought it a smart idea to climb over the feather edged perimeter fencing that surrounded the scout hut adjacent to the church opposite 3 Palmerston road. We were walking around the in the uncut grass surrounding the scout's hut when suddenly we were grabbed by a janitor and frog marched into the church and shoved down the cellar stair. While this was going on the janitor was swearing in adult searing and saying he was sick and tired of people trespassing on church property. He then stood us on a block of concrete in the corner of the cellar. Then as he walked off the cellar, he turned off the light. We were both crying uncontrollably with tears streaming down our faces. We thought we were going to die in that cellar. This man was out of control with rage, and we could hear his wife pleading with him not to do anything stupid. We thought this monster was going to kill us.

There are events in your life you find very difficult to forget. Well, this was one of them. We cried and cried until his wife came down the cellar stairs, unbeknown to her husband and opened the door to show us the way out. The side door we exited from is immediately opposite 3 Palmerston's front door. My mother was outside pacing up and down the street, frantically looking for both of us. We saw her and, crossed the road, and without looking, either way rushed straight into her arms with streams of tears running down our faces. We tried to tell Mom had happened, but the words failed to come out coherently.

Meanwhile, the janitor's wife walked over to explain how we had trespassed onto the church grounds. My mother looked at us then at the janitor's wife and said I hope these boys have not been harmed in any way or your husband will need to move neighbourhoods!! - we never heard anything after that little episode.

Ten years after that dreadful experience, when we had moved up to Hall Green – the church was burnt down. Perhaps the janitor had pushed his boat out too far this time?

CHAPTER 6 :
DADS FAMILY

My father was born the second son of ten children out of the union of Margaret Kelly, one of seven and John McEvilly, an only son. Their marriage was an arranged marriage because of necessity. John was in his forties and a bachelor sitting on one hundred and twenty acres of pasturable land. The majority of which was in fair condition for working wet farming. Margaret bore ten children, of which six were boys, and three were girls. Luckily, there were no child deaths but they were common in those days. In Ireland, farms with large families were not a sustainable. and, over the centuries many farms had become abandoned due to failure to provide an existence. Resulting in the majority of the inhabitants sailing across the Irish Sea for the bright lights of large UK cities, rather than stay happy though impoverished in the green emerald isle.

The Catholic church encouraged large families to strengthen its religious doctrine and, of course, to increase its coffers. What it didn't do was to help the population to educate themselves better in self-reliance and wealth creation. The power of the unelected church had over its flock was immense.

A fact laid bare at times if, for instance, you wanted your farm access road to receive tarmac, you would need to seek permission from the parish priest and in my Dad's farm, which was in

Plovervale, it took forty years for approval even though the collection of local rates/taxes for the church was realised. Dad told me power in Ireland was in the hands of the unelected parish priest. Frequent visits were made by priests to farmhouses was all too common. However, on one visit, the Parish Priest questioned my Grandfather John McEvilly's reduced offerings to the church plate the previous Sunday. My Grandfather went into a rage and told the priest having ten children, and following the church, teachings were offering's enough. He sent him away with a buzz in his earhole - perhaps that's why the road took so long to receive the must needed tarmac.

The nearby school, my father's siblings attended during his childhood, was called 'Log school'. It acquired its name because it had a similar shape to a log with no dividing walls between the classrooms. It was common practice for teachers to conducted several classes at any one time. My father left school at the grand age of fourteen with the achievement of obtaining the knowledge of the three R's which meant having the ability to apply fractions and decimals. The importance of education for the masses was not considered as significant by the Irish or British establishment as it is today. Perhaps they considered too much education was a threat to the establishment - better to keep the great-unwashed ill-informed because knowledge is a power. Once the maximum school age had been reached, the majority of children sought local employment. Farming was an option, though it was considered unsustainable. Dad managed to secure a job in ta large store in Castlebar. His older brother, John travelled further to Scotland to work on a hydro dam project. His venture abroad came to an abrupt ending when he had a nervous breakdown, and Dad was required to stand for twenty-four hours standing while travelling on numerous trains to the high lands of Scotland to bring him back to Mayo. There afterwards, my father was the man of the family once his father passed away due to an all too common heart attack.

The Barrett family of Breaffy had three sons who lived on

the nearby farm next to Plovervale. They attended the same school as my father and were classmates of the McEvilly's. After leaving school at an early age, the Barrett's went on to have successful careers. The youngest of them went off to build a large plant hire company called 'Motorways plant Ltd' providing the majority of plant hire for the construction of Britain's motorways. Walter Barrett became a director of 'George Wimpey Ltd' a construction company formed in 1880 and subsequently purchased in 1905 for five thousand pounds by a man called Sir Geoffrey Mitchell. The company went on to help the WW2 war effort by constructing ninety airdromes. One of which my father worked on for a short period after working on farms in Lincolnshire picking potatoes with other Mayo families like the Carneys and the Gallaghers. After WW2 during the 1950s and 60s, Wimpey went on to construct thousands of homes using 'no fines concrete' technique. This entailed the construction of many thousands of houses throughout the country with walls made of concrete having no sand in the concrete mix only aggregate and cement. This method of quick construction created thousands of homes and apartments for people living in slums up and down the country. The initiative was brought about by the then Wilson socialist government housing program. Walter Barrett became Managing director as a reward for his efforts in encouraging thousands of Irishmen from the free state to assist in the war effort against the Nazi regime. Walter found it necessary to alter his surname name from Barrett to Barr because he was a Catholic. No Catholics were allowed membership to the Masonic Temple. A secret society controlling most of Britain's business. These were remarkable achievements when you consider the limited education both Walter and his brother had.

CHAPTER 6 :
EMIGRATION

Large families struggling to make a living from the impoverished land in the west of Ireland sacrificed their sons so they could migrate to England and other parts of the globe in search of a better life, providing them opportunities to earn monies to remit. In England's large cities Irishmen had lonely lives due to their shyness and their inability to communicate with the English females caused by their thick 'brogues'.

They were frequently ridiculed by the English. Jokes about the 'Thick Irish' were familiar to those who thought they were funny. The insult was created by the English London press to blame the Irish for the 'potato blight' resulting in the Great famine in 1845, saying they started it because if their 'incompetence' in farming the land. However, this was untruthful.This situation resulted in many Irishmen remaining bachelors which must have been a very lonely life without a soul mate.Dad had five brothers. Only acquired himself a wife. He migrated to Canada and then onto California, the land of opportunity. And he certainly proved it was. He had eight children identical to my father, five daughters and three sons. His five daughters read Law at respectable universities, which possibly proves the saying that 'America is the land of opportunity'. Dad always said when an Irishman leaves Ireland, he leaves his heart behind. I suppose there are far more songs about Ireland itself, and fewer love songs about relatives or girlfriends left behind.

Printed in Great Britain
by Amazon

60874471R00104